THE BETTER JOHN GUIDE—
WHERE TO GO IN NEW YORK

JONATHAN ROUTH
with SERENA STEWART

The Better John
Guide—*Where to go*
in New York

Graffiti by John Glashan

G. P. Putnam's Sons

NEW YORK

To all those people with nowhere to go
(and whose need is greater than ours)

THIS IS AN IMPARTIAL GUIDE

Our visits to johns have been anonymous. We have not declared ourselves even after making use of the establishment's facilities.

Nor have we at any time accepted hospitality, but paid cash for all chargeable facilities we have used.

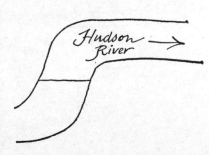

"This is the biggest waste of water
in the country by far. You spend
half a pint and flush two gallons."

—HRH Prince Philip, Duke of Edinburgh

"ENJOY YOURSELF!"

—Old Manhattan street cry

Contents

*

9

Johns of the East Forties

Johns of the West Fifties

Johns of the East Fifties

11

West Side Johns

The Johns of Central Park

Johns West of Central Park

Johns East of Central Park

The Johns of Upper Manhattan

13

Men, Women . . .
*

OUR PURPOSE

By bringing to your attention johns which you may not have realized existed, by drawing attention to amenities you may not have known they possessed, we hope to make your day in New York a more comfortable one.

In planning a walk from, say, Battery Park to the Oriental Department of New York Public Library; or from the Hayden Planetarium to the West Side YWCA, you will find that reference to the BETTER JOHN GUIDE will relieve you of many of the worries that beset the long-distance walker and tourist. *Plan your route by the Guide.* And please, if you make any interesting findings on the way, make use of the form at the end of the Guide.

We have not by any means included all johns that you will be passing. We decided, for instance, that it might not be in the public interest for us to recommend subway johns to persons who might be strangers to the ways of this city. Many of them are hard to find once you get into a station, many are not very clean, and most are very dull architecturally. And we have included very few of the johns run by the Parks people because they're pretty dull, too—though very nearly everywhere you come across a reasonable-sized patch of green you'll find one

15

of their branches. We haven't included theatre or cinema johns—but that is out of consideration for your purse. There's little point in paying $4.98 or $11.50 to get into one of these buildings when the amenity you want may be had in some adjacent building for free, or at the most 10¢.

GRADING OF JOHNS

Time and again we have set foot in an establishment which for hygiene just can't be faulted, and yet somehow it's just deadly dull; there's relief but no real pleasure to be had from visiting it.

Consequently our method of grading is based not just on a john's cleanliness, or its state of repair, or the efficiency of its fittings, or the friendliness of its staff, but also on its *atmosphere*, on the appeal of its immediate surroundings, and above all on how *enjoyable* a visit to it turns out.

This way it also makes more sense in comparing the merits of some johns in a deluxe hotel with those of a simple Park outhouse. And on these grounds this is how our grading works:

★ Interesting but not necessarily a temple to hygiene

★★ More than adequate hygienically and with atmosphere

★★★ Very well worth while traveling out of your way to visit

★★★★ Really outstanding in its own field

(Note, please, that at some addresses containing more than one set of johns this star grading may not apply to all sets of johns. And at other addresses it may apply to the john of one sex only, not to the set of johns.)

Could you please direct me to the nearest Men's Room?

I wouldn't even MISDIRECT you.

18

OUR FINDINGS

What struck us most about the johns of New York was their *dullness*. When one considers the incredible variety of décors in restaurants, museums, hotels around town, it's very sad to find that this décor has stopped short of their johns; that a dull hygienic sameness pervades so many of them. Just a few establishments—mostly high-class restaurants—have realized that hygiene and cleanliness do not have to be characterless; realized, perhaps, that a lot of their customers are going to file away their final and lasting impressions of the premises as a whole from the memory of their visit to its johns.

Johns are as necessary to our way of living as kitchens, as bedrooms, as front doors. And as such it's hypocritical to ignore them in the callous way they so often are treated, as the poor relation of the building.

The second thing which struck us in our travels was the total blind eye that New Yorkers seem set on turning toward their great heritage of Personal Hygiene and Cleanliness; the way they're just not interested in discovering, let alone perpetuating, the washroom habits of their past great.

For instance, we failed completely to locate Pierpont Morgan's Original John, the one he'd built his Library on East 36th St. to house along with his books, and which he used to visit via the underground passage from his house on 37th and Madison. It may still exist; but most likely not. All over New York it's the same. The johns of the great have been ripped out and consigned to the rubble-makers, and in their place characterless modern fittings installed. What an insight into the lives of some of these people if some of these treasures, as personal to them as their desks or beds, still existed. (And how right was Cubitt when he pronounced "You may judge a man by his company but better by the john he keeps.") How revealing to know what sort of tissue Morgan used (undoubtedly first-edition and hand-perforated if not actually signed by Henry Hand-Perforator himself); how equally revealing to know how many times per week he changed his scrubbing brush; or whether his porcelain was of Sèvres or Royal Doulton. According to the Lutherans who occupy his old house on 37th St., Morgan had a bath there twelve feet long and with gold taps. His john might well have been a john of the same size and splendor. But now we shall never know. Perhaps one day one of the companies which has grown rich through installing replacement fittings will feel it its duty to search out these treasures and establish premises where all may come to see and wonder at them. But at the rate this vandalism continues we may never see, never wonder. And New York's only real hygienic link with the past continues to be the small, indestructible Dyckman Commode (which see).

One final thing which struck us: this extraordinary preoccupation by the Managements of Johns with Hair Combers over Basins. Why should this body of unfortunates be singled out for such persecution in so many johns? They're not lesser Americans for the attention to their hair they like to give. And there's not a sink or drainage system in the land which would object to swallowing a few locks of the coarsest hair. Far better that it should fall in the sink and be swept away than on the floor where foreign feet might pick it up. The thought of Fifth Avenue, with hundreds of thousands of people whose shoes are matted with hair, tangling with each other, bringing each other stumbling to the ground, traffic all around them at a standstill because it cannot penetrate this vast jungle of hair which John Managements refuse to let be swept down their sinks, should be argument enough for them to revise this petty ruling.

. . . AND FINALLY

On our travels we heard many strange stories of johns.
Go and have a look at Mother Bertolottis' john in the
Village, people said. We did and saw nothing out of the
ordinary. Have a peep into Patricia Murphy's Candlelight john at midday, other people said. We did and again
peeped nothing out of the ordinary.

We were told of a place where not only the toilets are
fitted with chained Bibles but also there's one open at the
Text for Today above the Men's stalls. We were told of a
club where the only decoration in the Women's Room is
a full-sized photo of a naked man with a hinged figleaf
covering a part of his anatomy. All the waiters and old
patrons of the place know that if this is lifted, the move-
ment sets off a series of very loud burglar alarm bells in
the restaurant. But the lady who's a stranger to the place
doesn't. And eventually she has to come back out of the
room to her table in the restaurant. Neither of these
places were we able to find.

We were told of the Men's Room in a Madison Avenue block of offices which flushes a charming antibac-
teriological cerulean blue. Unfortunately we weren't told
about it before we'd used it, and very nearly had heart
failure.

We met a lady who told this story about her husband.
That one evening they were at the theatre, seated in their
box. He told her in the middle of one act that he was going to the john and walked out of the box. He wandered

23

down various corridors looking for it, couldn't find any attendants to guide him, and so when he finally turned his fiftieth corner and came across an aspidistra pot he made use of it.

He returned to his box and asked his wife, "Dear, what happened on stage while I was away?"

"You should know," she told him. "You were there."

Finally, our own true story. We'd gone to one establishment to inspect its johns and found them roped off on account they were flooded. So we went to the young lady at the information desk of the building and asked, "Couldn't we please just go down and *see* the rooms?"

Her face contorted and she ran to the back of the office. "Frank," she called into an inner room, "Come quick! I've got a couple of *perverts* here!"

Glossary

*

Just so there is no misunderstanding over the terms used in this Guide, this is what we mean by them:

John: The room in which a number of articles concerned with one's personal hygiene are situated and always including a toilet. The word originated with a student of that name at Harvard in 1735 who spent his whole time relieving the call of nature. Also referred to as the lavatory, the bathroom, the little boy's room, the rest room, the comfort station, the tinkle station, the bog (Irish), the loo (English).

A set of johns: one for men, one for women.

Toilet: Equipment for being seated upon, which, after use, is flushed.

Stall: Equipment designed for use by a gentleman in a standing position. Referred to as Urinal in plumbing circles.

Basin: Equipment fitted with taps at which the hands may be washed. Sometimes known as "sink."

NOTE: The order of johns in each section of the Guide is from south to north; i.e., anything on 42nd St. comes before anything on 43rd St.

25

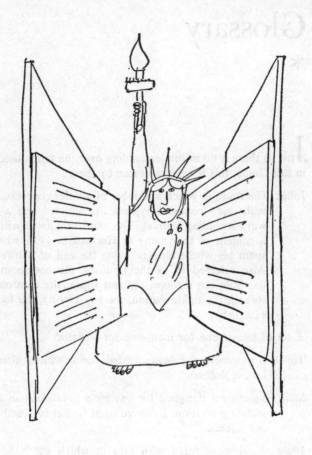

THE JOHNS
OF LOWER MANHATTAN

The LIBERTY ISLAND JOHNS

It strikes right where it hurts most to discover that the Statue of Liberty is not plumbed.* It just seems so frugal of the French. Where else in the world would you find a statute this size which isn't fitted with all the modern conveniences? Who else but the French, who we've always suspected of being a pretty mean lot, would be capable of making such a halfhearted and insulting gesture?

We submit that once all full-blooded Americans take in the enormity of this omission, once they realize that there is more wasted space in this statue than in any other building in New York in which johns which could be the envy of the whole free world could be installed, they will feel like us that the strongest possible representations should be made to France to replace the existing statue with a properly fitted one. Or this one should be sent back to France for some reputable Parisian plumbing firm to finish off the job properly.

The nearest johns for anyone caught short in the Statue

---

* According to one report, possibly put out by the French in self-defense, in Bartholdi's original designs there were going to be johns in it. The narrow balcony just under the torch was to do duty as a French open-style Men's pissoir; Women had a Room about stomach level with the Statue's navel serving as a window.

at present are the **All-American Johns** attached to the snack bar the other end of Liberty Island. The **Women's Room** has 11 free toilets and 6 h. & c. basins; the **Men's Room** 10 stalls, 4 free toilets, 4 h. & c. basins. You might just as well give the Statue a miss on any trip you take to the Island and go straight to these.

The LIBERTY ISLAND FERRY JOHNS

There are also of course johns on the ferry that plies between Battery Park and Liberty Island (leaves Pier 1 on the hour every hour 9 A.M. to 4 P.M.; in the summer to 5 P.M.). The round trip in these johns costs 90¢ for adults, 40¢ for children under 11. The **Women's Room** has 4 unusually shaped free toilets (no seats on 2), and 2 h. & c. basins (water unfit for drinking though). The **Men's Room** has 2 stalls, 2 free toilets and 2 h. & c. basins (water also unfit for drinking). Both these johns are above water level, both are decorated in shades of bilious green and yellow, and both—which is a very unique feature for New York johns—have portholes; 2 for Men, 3 for Women.

Knowing, as you now do, the scandalous facts concerning the lack of johns in the Statue of Liberty, you may prefer to stay in Battery Park and simply observe others making the unrewarding trip there. In that case you yourself will be in a position to visit:

The BATTERY PARK JOHNS

A. At the north end of the Park, a small building on the Green which has doors reminiscent of a bank's vault and which are open from 8 to 5. The **Women's Room** has 4 free toilets and 2 cold-water basins (no soap or towels); the **Men's Room** has 4 stalls, 2 free toilets, 2 cold-water basins and a large cupboard which we'll swear had a woman in it when we were there. No note was pushed under the door reading "Help! I am a prisoner in a Battery Park john!" so presumably she was quite happy.

B. South end of the Park, a small building near the playground, open the same hours and with similar accommodation to the other johns, but no signs of any women in cupboards in the **Men's Room.** (Nor any men in cupboards in the **Women's Room.**) Adjoining this is a special Children's john with 2 free toilets, 1 cold-water basin.

Both these sets of johns are of fairly recent construction so it's no good getting excited thinking they'd have been the ones first used by Dutchmen on arrival in Manhattan. Even 200 years ago the land on which they were built did not exist, but was still water.

If you are in this neighborhood after the Battery Park johns close then you can use:

The STATEN ISLAND FERRY TERMINAL JOHNS (open 24 hours)

You will see them clearly marked once you have paid your 5¢ at the turnstiles (which also entitles you to use the johns on the ferry).

Women: 8 toilets (5 at 5¢, 3 free and all of them very clean), 6 h. & c. basins (but no apparent soap or towels). Restriction: Combing and Spraying of Hair Forbidden—applies to outer room only.

Men: 6 stalls, 5 toilets (3 at 5¢, 2 free), 4 h. & c. basins, no apparent persecution of hair combers or sprayers.

The FERRY JOHNS THEMSELVES (or at any rate the johns on the John F. Kennedy ferry)

Women: (on foot passengers' boarding deck, starboard side—we think) 7 free toilets, 4 h. & c. basins (no apparent soap or towels), attendant usually only on between 6 A.M. and 10 P.M. Rather stuffy and disinfectant smelling. Restriction: (in outer room) "Please do not bring Food in here." Also a notice outside the room: "No Stretching out of Feet on Seats." You'd have to be very clever to do this.

Men: (turn right as you board and go downstairs, or belowdecks if you prefer it, and it's about half-way along on what we still think is the starboard side) 7 stalls, 4 free toilets (no doors), 4 cold-water basins. A pleasing use of aluminum here and really very much better value than places charging twice as much. Though, perhaps owing to its proximity to the engine room, it's quite one of the noisiest johns in the whole U. S. Notice outside the door: "Life Preservers will be found under Seats."—Not these seats.

The ST. GEORGE JOHNS (Ferry Terminal on Staten Island, also open 24 hours, but you'll have to pay a further 5¢)

Women: 15 toilets (10 at 5¢, 5 free), 8 h. & c. basins (signs that there might once have been soap and towel fixtures), same restrictions on hair combing and spraying as at the other terminal johns so remember to indulge yourself while afloat if you have to.

Men: 15 stalls, 10 toilets (5 at 5¢, 5 free), 6 h. & c. basins and a box marked "For Trash Only."

As to which of these three sets of johns you use it's really a question of time. You're going to have to pay 5¢ anyway. The ferry is a rarer experience than the terminals and if you don't want to have to do the round trip in the johns and have to get off the other end, it is just possible to get on the ferry, visit the johns and rush off before it sails. Alternatively, why not have yourself a ball and use all three?

★ GEORGE WASHINGTON'S FAREWELL JOHN

Fraunces Tavern, corner of Broad and Pearl Streets

We quote from the official guide: "On the 4th of December, 1783, General Washington bade the officers of the Continental Army good-bye while in Fraunces Tavern. Filling a glass with wine, after the ceremonious fashion of the time, he said: 'With a heart full of love and gratitude, I now take leave of you. I most earnestly wish that your latter days may be as prosperous and happy as your former ones have been glorious and honorable. I cannot come to each of you and take my leave, but shall be obliged to you, if each of you will come to me and take me by the hand.' 'Twas a sad time to those assembled. Washington left the room, passing through the Light Infantry, and walked . . ."

Well, we reckon after a night of wine like that he would then have walked upstairs to the third floor and availed himself of the amenities of the room marked **Gentlemen,** just beyond the picture of "Molly Pitcher at the Battle of Monmouth." They're certainly pretty old, the fittings: 2 stalls with high chain-operated cistern, basin with marble sideboard, and 2 Vortex Special toilets with French shutter-type double doors and also chain-operated cistern.

In the **Ladies** room on this floor there are 2 free toilets, and basin with—what is very rare in New York—real bar of soap. Also an outer rom with some gently dilapidated furnishings.

31

These 3rd-floor johns are both No-Smoking johns and are open Mon.–Fri. 10 to 4, Sat. 10 to 3. But there are other johns on the 1st floor between the bar and restaurant which appear to be open Mon.–Fri. 12 to 8, Sat. 12 to 3. Nothing of especial interest in them except the arrangement of the **Men's** toilets which instead of being side by side are one in front of the other.

In the 2nd-floor museum arranged by the Sons of the Revolution there is also a lock of George Washington's hair. It does not state whether this was retrieved after he had been combing it at a basin.

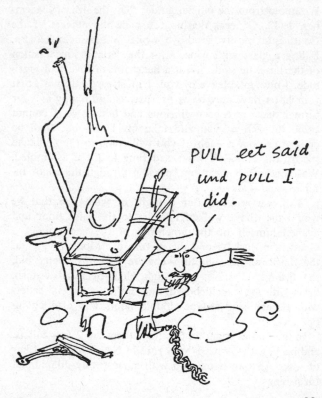

PULL eet said und PULL I did.

★★OSCAR'S DELMONICO JOHNS (installed 1835; replumbed mid-20th century)

Oscar's Delmonico Restaurant, corner of Beaver and William Sts. Open 11:30 to 9:30 Mon.–Sat.

Women: (between the two 1st-floor dining rooms) 2 free toilets, elegant marble-topped basin with gold-looking fittings, real soap and linen towels.

Men: (by the tickertape machine set just beyond the bar) 2 free toilets, 2 blue stalls, rather splendid double basin with soap and linen towels laid out. Crowded at lunch, but a quiet place for a leisurely wash in the evening.

Both establishments are small, but they're warm and very much more elegant than other competitive establishments in the area.

SLOPPY LOUIE'S JOHN

Sloppy Louie's, 92 South St.

A useful john to know if you're stuck in Fulton Fish Market between 8 A.M. and 8 P.M. weekdays. Upstairs and rather small. **Men's Room** just has room for 1 toilet, 1 man; basin outside. **Women's Room** beside it.

The STOCK EXCHANGE JOHNS

A. **The New York Stock Exchange Johns, 20 Broad St. (open Mon.–Fri. 10 a.m. to 3:30)**
Elevator to the 3rd floor and they're just before the Visitors Gallery. **Women's Room** has 3 free toilets, 3 basins, is very plain and very clean. **Men's Room** has 3 stalls, 5 free toilets, 2 h. & c. basins. Transactions are not encouraged to take place on this floor.

B. **The American Stock Exchange Johns, 86 Trinity Place (open Mon.–Fri. 10 a.m. to 3:30)**

Follow signs saying "To Visitors Gallery," pass through this gallery which overlooks the floor of the Exchange and the johns are in the Lounge off it; some of the most excitingly positioned johns in New York. Inside them you're conscious most of the noise from outside, like a battle going on with hundreds of people in dreadful agony. (They restrain their passions at the other Exchange.) It's not conducive to a long or restful stay however; but it's exciting. And we're fairly sure there's a plain-clothes detective positioned outside the doors. **Women's Room** has 3 free toilets, 2 basins. (No knowledge of hand signals necessary for communication with attendant.) **Men,** 4 stalls, 4 free toilets, 3 h. & c. basins. Next time your broker offers to meet you at your convenience suggest the pleasant communal lounge right here.

The CITY HALL JOHNS

City Hall, City Hall Park on Broadway and Chambers St. Open 9 to 4 weekdays

We know a lady who hankers for the lush life who regularly uses these johns three or four times a week even though it entails her traveling from the East Sixties to do so. She tells her husband or escort that she's got to see the Mayor for a minute—never explains what about—leaves him waiting in the hallway while she ascends the splendid circular staircase—which is the real attraction of the place to her—and in fact simply visits the **Ladies' Room** (4 free toilets, 3 h. & c. basins) on the second floor. Then she comes down the stairway again looking very important and splendid as anyone who uses the stairway properly must do and goes off back home. Well, everyone's entitled to their own beautiful experience. But

34

you won't get it if you're male because the **Men's Room** which, it has been said, is the real seat of power in this city, is downstairs in the basement by the air-conditioning plant (2 stalls, 3 free toilets, 2 h. & c. basins).

The JUDICIAL JOHNS

A. At the U. S. Courthouse, in Foley Square on Pearl St.

These are probably used by more innocent than guilty persons but they still manage to make an awful mess of the place. Make for U. S. District Court No. 1 and you'll see them marked at the end of the passage, either upstairs or down. We were told they were open 24 hours.

B. At New York County Courthouse, Centre and Pearl Sts.

Not the least attractive features of these johns is the approach to them after you enter the front door of the building. Walk to the base of the great dome and take the elevator to the 2nd floor. Walk a little

35

around the dome and take a narrow staircase up to the open gallery, find required door and walk down the steps inside it.—This may sound like nothing great but you'll be stunned by the vistas and the amount of marble you encounter en route. The **Women's Room** has 7 free toilets and 3 h. & c. basins. The **Men's Room,** 5 stalls, 6 free toilets, 3 h. & c. basins and a footbath (or maybe it's for washing your dirty linen in). Open normally weekdays 9 to 5 but also so long as the front door is open.

The CHINATOWN JOHNS

Out of an indifferent lot we would recommend a visit to the **Chinatown Fair Johns,** 7 Mott Street. At the end of the room, they're advertised as "Public Toilets—Clean and Sanitary." Pay 5¢ at a turnstile. **Women's Room** has 2 toilets, 1 basin and an injunction to "Kindly Keep Clean. Do not Write on Walls. Thank-you." (No restrictions on Combing Hair or Braiding Pigtails though.) **Men's Room** has 1 stall, 1 toilet, 1 cold-water basin. But there's little of the glamour or mystery of the Orient about either of them.

VILLAGE JOHNS

The WASHINGTON SQUARE JOHNS

The building on the south side of the Square is one of the chain of johns run by the Parks people. 10 free toilets and 2 cold-water basins in the **Women's.** 11 stalls, 5 toilets (no seats or doors) and 1 cold-water basin in the **Men's.** A pretty miserable place. Open, 8 to 5.

The POLITICAL AND PORNOGRAPHIC JOHNS

Café Figaro, 186 Bleecker St. (corner of MacDougal St.)

The johns here are a must for anyone who wants to keep up with what's new in graffiti. They have some good political writers with strong views on Vietnam; some very dull pornographic correspondents. (Why can't they ever think of anything *new* to write? One of the best is still "I am 9½ inches long. Anyone interested?" underneath which someone else had written: "Not just interested. *Fascinated*. How long is your ——?") On the edition of the walls we saw there were one or two publishable items: "Pinkey Lee is secretly alive in Argentina." "Dave Bromberg is more fun than a National Park." (That was in the **Women's Room**). "I am the rightful heir to President Poke yet no one will listen to me." "Trotsky will Return." "To be Beat is to be cool. To be beat-cool is NOT to be Beat. To be Beat-Cool and not to be beat is

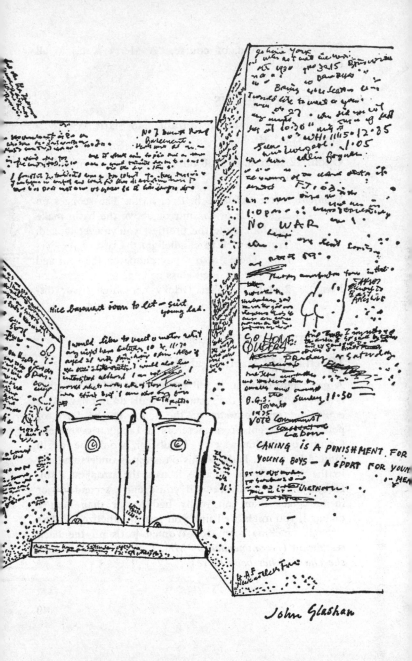

John Glashan

NOWHERE." And, of course, "A Merry Xmas to all our Readers."

★
W

O. HENRY'S JOHNS

O. Henry's Bar and Restaurant, 345 Sixth Ave. (corner of West 4th St.)

Open: 12:00 p.m. to 1:30 a.m. Mon.–Sat., to midnight Sun.

Women: 2 free toilets, 1 h. & c. basin. The sconces on either side of the mirror above the basin make you look quite the prettiest you've ever looked. Try and stick to candlelight the rest of the evening. There's also a pay phone on the wall and a dropped stained-glass ceiling.

Men: 2 stalls, 1 toilet (tricky neck-high tissue dispenser), 1 h. & c. basin. Plain ceiling.

MINETTA'S JOHNS

Minetta's, 113 MacDougal St.

A great pity that the pencil portraits of old and regular customers that deck the restaurant walls do not have their equivalent on the walls of the johns in the form of penciled comments from these old and regular customers. Graffiti by Hemingway or Lindbergh would be worth quite a bit today. Perhaps this omission is understandable in the **Men's Room** because it uses the strongest disinfectant known to man and if you spent a second longer in the place than you really had to, or than Nature dictated, you might well find yourself anesthetized. A less strongly smelling room for **Women** leads off the back restaurant (*recommended by Mrs. Leslie Perrin who says she changed her baby there*).

JOHNS JUST OFF
THE VILLAGE

★ **The OLD MERCHANT'S JOHNS**
The Old Merchant's House, 29 East 4th St.

The procedure for using these johns is as follows: First of all there are only certain times that you can be admitted to them, those advertised on the board outside, 1, 2, 3, and 4 o'clock on the hour and not on Mondays or Holidays. Go down the area steps beside this board and ring the doorbell. Then when the young lady opens the door to you follow her in, sign your name and address in the register she will give you, and pay her 50¢ (Children 25¢). You may now avail yourself of the following amenities (in the basement):

Women: 1 toilet, 1 h. & c. basin and a marble Victorian basin stand.

Men: (under the stairs) 1 stall, 1 basin, 1 hole in the floor.*

The truth is that this charming little museum (private house with contents unchanged since 1850) is short of funds. If only enough people could be encouraged to visit it the owners would be able to finish off the job of installing a toilet in the Men's Room and perhaps keep it

* Nearest john for men who need more than this, Lincoln's Great John at Cooper Union, which see.

41

open all day instead of just at selected hours. As it is, there's even danger that the Women's johns might fall down if these funds aren't forthcoming. So we feel it's up to all New Yorkers who care for the amenities of their city to support this cause either by paying their 50¢ to visit the place, or by sending a donation to:

> Save the Old Merchant's John Fund
> 29 East 4th St.
> N.Y.C.

★ LINCOLN'S GREAT JOHN
M

Cooper Union, Cooper Square (bounded by 3rd and 4th Aves., Astor Place and 7th St.)

The Great Hall of Cooper Union is where, on February 27, 1860, Abraham Lincoln made a speech which it has long been held opened the Presidential door for him. Probably before, or immediately after the chat another door was opened to him on the fifth floor of the building, leading into a room 16 feet high and containing 4 rather ancient stalls, 4 free toilets, 1 h. & c. basin and a view through the window of half the neighborhood. (Conversely, a view by half the neighborhood through the window. But a view of the neighborhood, by the neighborhood and for the neighborhood was just what would have attracted Lincoln to it.) This room, with contents as described, today bears no other plaque to commemorate the visit than the label on the door, **Men's Room.**

Mrs. Lincoln is more likely to have been taken to the fourth floor of the building to a room in a bilious shade of green containing 3 free toilets, 3 well-equipped basins and in the mornings, oodles of sunshine.

Both these johns, primarily intended for visitors to the Cooper Union Museum for the Arts of Decoration (open Mon.–Sat. 10 to 5, but closed Sat. June to Sept., admission free) are supported entirely by endowments and voluntary contributions and are not tax-supported. All contributions to their upkeep welcome, or if you'd like details of how you can endow a basin or toilet contact the Trustees.

McSORLEY'S WONDERFUL JOHN

McSorley's Old Ale House (Dorothy O'Connell Kirwan, Pres. Good Ale—Raw Onions—No Ladies) 15 East 7th St. (between 2nd and 3rd Aves.)

Open: Mon.–Sat. 8 a.m. to 1 a.m., Sun. 1 p.m. to midnight

Women: The problem does not arise.

Men: Straight through at the end of the bar, 3 jumbo-size stalls sixty years old with a wood-covered cistern operated by a piece of string over them, 2 toilets, tiny tucked-away basin. Regulars find it convenient anyway.

McSORLEY'S WONDERFUL JOHN

McSorley's Old Ale House (Dorothy O'Connell Antwan, Prop., Good Ale—Raw Onions—No Ladies) 15 East 7th St. (between 2nd and 3rd Aves.)

Open: Mon.-Sat. 8 a.m. to 1 a.m., Sun. 1 p.m. to midnight

Women: The problem does not arise.

Men: Straight through at the end of the bar, 3 panfor-size stalls sixty years old with a wood-covered cistern operated by a piece of string over them, 2 toilets, tiny tucked-away basin. Regulars find it convenient anyway.

JOHNS ABOVE THE VILLAGE

★★VICTOR HERBERT'S JOHNS (and just about everybody else's)

Luchow's, 110 E. 14th St. between 3rd and 4th Aves.

Open: Tues.–Sun. 11 a.m. to midnight, closed Mon.

These johns have been favorites among celebrities for two generations.

Women: (through to the back on the left-hand side) 3 free toilets (paintings of 19th-century ladies on doors), 2 h. & c. basins, ornate dressing table, chandeliers, floral carpeting, red fabric walls. Very lush though possibly more reproduction than genuine. **Extra:** pay phone.

Men: (in the construction situated on the middle of the restaurant floors, entry just past the cash desk in the Gentlemen's Grill) 5 stalls, 3 free toilets, 2 h. & c. basins, stained-glass roof. Skilled attendant will be happy to assist you in your choice of many lotions available on the shelves.

THEODORE ROOSEVELT'S FIRST JOHN

Theodore Roosevelt's Birthplace, 28 East 20th St.

Open: Daily, 9 to 4:30. (Admission 25¢, children under 12 free)

45

There are small but adequate johns in the basement, both with wood-paneled outer rooms—a cot in the **Women's**. Unlikely that Roosevelt ever used either of them however. Far more probably he had a potty in the 2nd-floor nursery. A locked cupboard between this room and the back bedroom may well hold the answer.

The POLICE ACADEMY JOHNS

Police Academy, 235 East 20th (between 2nd and 3rd Aves.)

It cost us $15 to use these johns. We took the elevator to the 4th floor. Room 216 just outside the entrance to the Police Museum was for **Women** (2 free toilets, 1 h. & c. basin), Room 217 for **Men** (4 free toilets with rather gay blue doors, 4 stalls, 3 h. & c. basins, electric shaver outlets). And contrary to what we might have expected from a brief glance into the Museum no attempt was made in the johns to molest us, push dope to us, kidnap us, murder us, pick our pockets or sell us a half share in the Brooklyn Bridge. We saw no sign of anyone having broken and entered, or of having attempted to pick any locks. There weren't even any slots on the toilet doors in which a counterfeiter could have used up his homemade money. There was no net spread out below the window which could have broken our fall if we'd tried to commit suicide. The only sign of crime we saw was of our own doing; stuck on the windshield of the car we'd been rash enough to park outside the building during our ten-minute visit. And that is why we remember these as the most expensive johns in the city.

★★CAVANAGH'S JOHNS
W

Cavanagh's Restaurant, 260 West 23rd St. (between 7th and 8th Aves.)

Open: Sun.–Fri. 12 p.m. to 11 p.m., Sat. 5 p.m. to 11 p.m.

Our visit here established the fact that a lady wearing slacks may use the john even though at the same time she may be barred, on account of this mode of dress, from

47

using the place's eating facilities.* Despite the resentment we may have felt at the time we have to admit it's a very pretty **Ladies' Room**—upstairs to the right of the front entrance, and pink and clean like most of the people who patronize the place, 3 free toilets, 2 h. & c. basins, outer room with good makeup counter. The **Men's Room** at the back on the 1st floor, just inside the parking lot entrance, has 2 stalls, 1 free toilet, 1 h. & c. basin.

The CHELSEA JOHNS

Hotel Chelsea, 222 West 23rd St. (between Seventh and Eighth Aves.)

Men: (main entrance and turn right) 1 stall, 1 free toilet, 1 h. & c. basin. Used by Brendan Behan, Dylan Thomas, Thomas Wolfe.

Women: (back of lobby and turn right) 1 free toilet, 1 h. & c. basin. Used by Brendan Behan, Dylan Thomas, Thomas Wolfe.

---

* The reason given, very gently but firmly, for not being allowed to dine in slacks was that this was a "house." We don't follow either.

JOHNS OF THE
WEST THIRTIES

The MISSING PENNSYLVANIA STATION JOHNS

Pennsylvania Station, bounded by 31st and 33rd Sts., Seventh and Eighth Aves.

Will whoever took these johns please return them to the above address.

HORACE GREELEY'S JOHNS (sometimes mistakenly referred to as the HERALD SQUARE JOHNS)

Beneath the statue of Horace Greeley in Greeley Square at junction of Broadway, Sixth Ave. and W. 33rd St. (if you can ever get across the street)

Women: 5 free toilets (no seats nor have there ever been), 3 cold-water basins, no soap, no towels.
Men: 7 stalls, 12 free toilets (no doors, no seats), 1 cold-water basin, 1 drinking fountain.

These johns exist for use in dire emergency only. The **Men's** particularly has a very weird reputation, which may or may not have something to do with its graffiti. One scrawled sentence read "Do you like Grils?"—underneath which someone else had scrawled "Do you mean *Girls?*"—underneath which the original writer

(presumably) had written "What's wrong with us Grils?"
Another scrawled sentence ran "I have two of everything.
What shall I do with them?" And beneath that another
hand had written "I should buy some books." This place
seems to specialize in writers who collaborate on their
graffiti.

MACY'S JOHNS

Macy's, Broadway to 7th Ave. between 34th and
35th Sts.

Open: 9:45 to 6 (to 9 Mon., Thurs. and Fri.)

These are the ones we found:

1. On the lower level near the Home Cleaning Center: a
   Women's Room with 23 toilets (10 free, 13 at 10¢)
   10 h. & c. basins and 5¢ mechanical foot massage
   vibrator. **Men's Room** with 4 stalls, 10 toilets (3 free,
   7 at 10¢), 6 h. & c. basins.

2. On the 4th floor, Broadway side of the store near the Little Sister Shop, a **Women's Room** with 8 regular toilets (3 free and 5 at 10¢) and 3 other paired toilets —one beside the other, one smaller than the other; presumably for children with nannies. Also 10 h. & c. basins, three of which are lower than the others.

3. On the 6th floor on the 7th Avenue shop, near Women's Shoes one way and Needlepoint and Rug-making the other, Macy's **Main Women's Room.** 67 toilets (is this a record?—28 free and 39 at 10¢, seat covers available for an extra 5¢), 35 h. & c. basins. **Extras:** Penny Scale, 5¢ Mechanical Foot Massage Vibrator, Change Machine.

4. On the 8th floor by the Patio Restaurant, a **Women's Room** with 6 free toilets, 6 h. & c. basins. A **Men's Room** with 2 stalls, 3 free toilets, 3 h. & c. basins.

If we were making use of a sign meaning "Not worth going out of your way to visit unless you are overcome with a desperate urge to indulge in a little foot massage" it would be about the only thing we could put alongside Macy's johns. And possibly also another sign meaning "The 4th-floor johns are cleaner than the others."

GIMBEL'S JOHNS

Gimbel's, Broadway and 33rd St. on Herald Square

Open: 9:45 to 6 (to 9 Mon., Thurs., Fri.)

The ones recommended on the store directory are:

Women: 3rd floor by the Post Office with sign outside reading "Loitering and Soliciting in this building prohibited." 28 toilets (9 free, 1 for children only, 18 at 5¢) 10 h. & c. basins. Outer room with chairs, penny scale, soft drink, cigarette and candy dispensers, luggage checking

51

lockers and pay phones. A better bargain than Macy's really.

Men: 2nd floor through Men's Clothing by the escalators. 1 stall, 25¢ toilets, 2 h. & c. basins. Nobody, but nobody would want to make a habit of going here.

The EMPIRE STATE JOHNS

Empire State Building, Fifth Ave. and 34th St.

There may well be others, but the only ones we could find were some tiny cramped ones on the 86th floor, which cost us each $1.75 to get to (open 9:30 A.M. to midnight); and those on the first floor in the Mark Twain Riverboat Restaurant. The **Women's** here has 2 free toilets, 1 basin, is small, clean and smells exactly like bubble gum. The **Men's,** also free, has a wallpaper which shows Alarmed Peasants Shooting a Giant Vegetable. In other words it's much better, and infinitely cheaper, to keep your feet firmly on the ground than your head up in the clouds if caught short in this building. Though if it's any consolation to you as you use the $1.75 basin on the 86th floor or if it gives you any sense of achievement, the dirty water you're letting out of it has a longer downward journey to make than any other dirty water in any other building in the world. Some may feel it a proud boast to make.

There is definitely no john on the 102nd-floor observation roof.

JOHNS OF THE EAST THIRTIES

PIERPONT MORGAN'S GUEST JOHNS

Pierpont Morgan Library, 29 E. 36th St. (between Madison and Park Aves.)

Open: 9:30 to 5:00 daily, closed Sun. and August. Free admission

Women: Ask the attendant to escort you—not that this is country where you're likely to be attacked —but the room is so tastefully labeled you might otherwise miss it. Go through a series of 3 separate paneled doors and you will find 3 free toilets, 2 h. & c. basins. Spotless.

Men: You may also need an attendant to escort you if the room is locked. He has the key. Inside: nothing worth stealing, just 1 stall, 2 free toilets, 2 h. & c. basins. Also spotless.

The EAST SIDE AIR JOHNS

East Side Airlines Terminal, First Ave. and 37th St.

Open: 24 hours

Women: 18 toilets (2 free, 16 at 10¢), 16 h. & c. basins. Outer room for makeup, also cradle and crib.
Extras: Penny scale, pay phones, Automatic

53

Merchant dispensing Aspirin, Nail Clippers, Lipstick, Hand Lotion, Toothbrush and Toothpaste, Perfume, Handkerchief, Comb-all at 25¢, and Kleenex at 10¢.

Men: 16 stalls, 20 10¢ toilets and 1 free, 25 h. & c. basins. **Extras:** soft music, 2 penny scales, coin changer, 3 shoeshine seats at 25¢ (or dyed $1.50), pay phones, and Automatic Merchant dispensing Shave Cream Cartridge, Luggage Label Holder, Emergency Shave Kit, Aspirin, Souvenir Pen, Toothbrush and Toothpaste, Comb, Handkerchief, Hair Tonic and "Delilah" Perfume at 25¢, and Kleenex at 10¢.—A night out here could quite easily set you back $3 to $4.

There is free transportation every fifteen minutes from these johns to the johns at Grand Central Station; and frequent connections to the johns at Kennedy Airport (bus fare $1.75).

JOHNS OF THE
WEST FORTIES

The PUBLIC LIBRARY or CIRCULATING JOHNS

New York Public Library, Fifth Ave. and 42nd St.

Open: Mon.–Sat. 9 a.m. to 10 p.m., Sun. 1 p.m. to 10 p.m.

A. On the ground floor. Room 77, by the door to the Fallout Shelter just inside the 42nd St. entrance to the building, is also marked **Señoras and Women's Room.** 7 toilets (2 at 10¢ with mirrors and purse racks, 5 free without mirrors but with collapsing metal purse racks), 2 h. & c. basins and enormous hand-drying machine. Restrictions: No Smoking. Hair Combing is Prohibited in this Room. Also, which should perhaps be mentioned under this heading, a pile of pamphlets immediately outside the door saying "Readers, please note for your convenience, the Library regrets that it is not possible to make seating space available for studying books which visitors bring with them."

B. On the 3rd floor. There is a **Women's and Señoras Room** in Room 306 just before Rare Books. 10 toilets (3 at 10¢, 7 free), 4 h. & c. basins, no apparent persecution of hair combers.

C. On the 3rd floor, but the other side of the building to

the Women's Room, is Room 325 (near the Berg Collection) marked **Men and Caballeros.** 8 toilets (5 at 10¢ with doors, 3 free without), 4 stalls, 3 h. & c. basins, and a window very useful for spying on who's orientating whom in the Oriental Department on the 2nd floor.

Where,
Oh Where,
Can I comb,
My hair?

It was in one of the 10¢ toilets in the Men's Room that we first saw the slogan, which kept reappearing on the walls of similar establishments in the city, "Abramowitz is a Neo-Classicist" (and a nastier or filthier thing to say about Abramowitz one can't conceive). Scrawled very viciously, it was. The only reading matter in the entire place. But apart from this all the johns in this building were conspicuously if not exceptionally clean.

The BRYANT PARK DISGUSTING MEN'S JOHN

Bryant Park, behind the Public Library, between 40th and 42nd Sts.

This is a small Greek-temple-type place not far from the 42nd St. entrance to the Library, with 10 stalls, 3 toilets (no doors), 3 cold-water basins (no mirrors, no towels), and a widely ignored notice requesting No Spitting, No Loitering. Not at all a place for scholars and others of a sensitive nature, who should make for the Library as fast as possible if they find themselves in the neighborhood.

The TIMES SQUARE or TOFFENETTI JOHNS

Toffenetti's Restaurant, corner of Broadway and 43rd (The man at the Dept. of Commerce Information Center in Times Square advised us these were the best and most conveniently placed johns in the area.)

These johns put on quite a show. Go down the stairs to the back of the basement restaurant:

Women: In the inner room, 4 toilets (2 free, 2 at 10¢ but no difference), 4 h. & c. basins, 3 hand-drying machines. Outer room, 8 pink chairs and makeup ledges. **Extras:** Automatic dispensing machine selling Lipstick; another Scent, Jumping Beans, Cigarette Holders, Sewing Kit, Alka-Seltzer—all at 25¢; and penny scale with built-in Question and Answer mechanism—you set the Question (Do men like me? How many locks has the Suez Canal? Where

59

will I meet my Master? Whom can I best Dominate? I dreamed I was mad . . . I dreamed of pigs . . . When was VJ Day? Do I have many Admirers?) and the machine gives you the Answer (like "Not as many as you think," or "Your Moods dominated you").

Men: Outer room with shoe-cleaning seat and non-Answering penny scale. Inner room, 3 stalls, 3 h. & c. basins, 4 toilets (2 free, 2 at 10¢, again no difference; but like the ones in the Women's they're a little bit frightening if you've never experienced them before. The toilet seat is actually plugged into an electric socket and is lit up just like a pinball table. According to the directions, it's an Ultraviolet Sterilamp that's making the seat germ-free after each use—"sanitized in 60 seconds." Quite a spectacle.) **Extras** here: one machine selling pocket combs at 10¢; another ("The Mechanical Servant") giving choice of Nail Clippers, Bird Whistle, Automatic Cigarette Ejector Holder, Diamond Ring ("Adjustable, Simulated"), Pocket Knife with Bottle Opener and Screw Driver, Playful Dogs with Magnetic Action ("They're tricky, entertaining") or Shrunken Head ("Hang in Car") at 25¢. Who wants to traipse out to Coney Island when there's all this in the center?

SARDI'S JOHNS

Sardi's Restaurant, 234 West 44th St. (between Broadway and Eighth Ave.)

Open: Mon.–Sat. 11 a.m. to 2 a.m.

Small free adequate johns at the head of the stairs which attract a pretty smart clientele. Priority given during the early evening to patrons who have a show to make.

★★The ASTOR JOHNS

M

Astor Hotel, 1515 Broadway (between 44th and 45th Sts.—or it was, anyway).

Women: (lower level) 4 toilets (1 free, 3 at 10¢), 4 h. & c. basins, carpeted outer room for makeup but hold your lipstick firm when the subway's operating.

Men: 10 stalls, 1 free and 12 10¢ toilets, 10 h. & c. oval basins arranged rather picturesquely in the center of the room with free shave talc and lotions, hairbrush and comb. Also shoeshine service at 30¢. Quite a pleasing old-fashioned atmosphere about this place.

The Astor johns are extremely popular among theatregoers during Intermissions. Sometimes, when really popular shows are playing, you may feel it best to try to make a reservation. But regret, no mail-order bookings: personal callers only.

★★★The JOHNS OF THE TWELVE CAESARS

Forum of the Twelve Caesars, 57 West 48th St.

Open: daily, noon to 3 and 6 to 10. Patronized by Senators and advertising centurions

Feminae et Virginae: (down the stairs) II free toiletariums, II h. & c. basins (gold taps, and a faucet depicting a boy on a piece of celery, or possibly dolphin). On the marble dressing tables in the outer room IV sets of Chanel toilet water sprays, IV Chanel scents, I Madame Rochas and I Femme. Also genuine Récamier, phone and daily papers. Everything pink and gray marble wherever possible, but the whole effect is Deuxième Empire rather than Roman Empire.

62

Homines: (down the stairs) So elegant it seems almost insulting to use the terms stalls, toilets or basins (but there are II of each, and the basins have gold Caesar-head taps and a raised gold soap dish with a soft pad inside so the soap doesn't get bruised). Really one expects to find a bath and slaves and clean-limbed Nubians to brush one down. The attendant does his best though.

The ROCKEFELLER JOHNS

Rockefeller Centre, 48th to 51st St. on Fifth and Sixth Aves.

A. **The Basement Johns** (open 8:30 A.M. to 8:30 P.M.) Entering by 30 Rockefeller Plaza go down to the basement and take a long walk past the shops to the end of the corridor, **Men** to the left, **Women** to the right. Both sets of johns cost 10¢ to use, payable into a turnstile on entry. The **Women** have 16 toilets and 7 basins and an attendant in nurses uniform. The **Men** can accommodate 8 standing, 6 seated, and 5 at basins. A hygienic but slightly prisonlike atmosphere pervades.

B. **The 70th-Floor Johns** (open 9 A.M. to midnight daily) These are attached to the observation deck of the RCA Building and although Free to use there's what might be termed a cover charge of $1.35 just getting there. The **Women** has 2 toilets, 1 basin and a very stiff entrance door. The **Men** has 1 toilet, 2 stalls, and 1 h. & c. basin. It's very clean, very hot, and the view through the glass window of the door (of the Men's only) right across Central Park is a lot preferable to what greets you outside the door of the Basement Johns.

C. There are free johns in both the **English Grill** and **French Room Restaurants** (open 11:30 A.M. to 9:30 P.M.) on the Lower Plaza by the Skating Rink. Nothing very spectacular, except the French ones are labeled **Mesdames** and **Messieurs,** and the English **Ladies** goes in for leather armchairs. There is also a small **Ladies Only John** by the skating rink changing rooms.

D. **The Rainbow Grill Johns** (open 6 P.M. to 2 A.M. Mon.–Sat.) attached to the Rainbow Grill, 65th floor of the RCA Building. These are nothing very special.

★★★E. **The Rainbow Room Johns** (open 4 P.M. to 2 A.M.
M   Mon.–Sat.) attached to the Rainbow Room, 65th floor
★★   of the RCA Building. The **Men's Room** here (turn
W   left inside entranceway, past the checkroom and up a tiny flight of stairs) has the most fabulous view of any john in New York, a view right across the city which you are actually able to appreciate while using the standing facilities of the room. Why pay to visit the 70th-floor Observation Deck when this can be had for free? Also free are the lotions over the basins, including one called Fabergé's Cologne Aphrodisia. Makes a great start to any evening. The **Women's Room** (left inside entranceway in an alcove) has no view, alas; plenty of marble including marble shelves covered in useful cosmetics (powder, face cream, makeup removing cream, Fabergé scent sprays), masses of linen, a lot of useful things like safety pins (indeed, the whole place is geared to people doing running repairs of one sort or another) and a charming attendant who puts on white gloves to hand you your towel at the basin. Tip 25¢ (and one day try to get a peep into the Men's Room).

JOHNS OF THE
EAST FORTIES

★★★The GRAND CENTRAL JOHNS

Grand Central Station, East 42nd St. between Vanderbilt and Lexington Aves.

Open: 24 hours

These rank among the great johns of the modern world, not so much palaces of hygiene as of pleasure in which the toilet facilities take second place to the other attractions present. There are 2 main sets of johns:

A. The Upper Level Johns

Women: An outer room with writing tables, benches, chairs, rocking chairs, 6 pay phones, a 25¢ Photograph-Yourself machine, a 10¢ machine dispensing The Lord's Prayer as a Lucky Charm Medal, a series of 25¢ luggage lockers, a 15¢ cold drink machine, a 25¢ "Mechanical Servant" dispensing Lipstick, Perfume, Toys, Alka-Seltzer, Toothpaste, Pen, Manicure Set, Aspirin, Comb, Bobby Pins, Kleenex. In the inner room, 28 toilets (5 free, 23 at 10¢), 22 h. & c. basins (mirrors over and ledges for makeup but no chairs; also choice of electric hand drier or 5¢ towel dispenser). **Extras** in machines: combs or Kleenex at 10¢, perfume or lipstick at 25¢. Normally kept extremely clean and with a most helpful attendant. Also side room with 12 25¢

dressing rooms (basin, toilet, mirror, soap, towel) and 1 fitted with nursery facilities.

Men: In the approach hallway, pay phones, barber shop, 7 25¢ shoeshines (50¢ for white and suede shoes, 50¢ for the saddlesoap special, 35¢ for shoes scoured). In the main room:

- man-operated booth where you can get Suits Pressed While-U-Wait (75¢)
- another man-operated booth where you can get Hats Cleaned and Blocked (50¢) New Lining ($1) New Sweat Band (50¢)
- change machine
- penny scale
- Brylcreem dispenser (5¢)
- "Mechanical Servant" dispensing Nail Clippers, Charms, Hanky, Tricky Dogs, Toothbrush, Deodorant, Pocket Knife (all 25¢)
- another machine dispensing Kleenex, Alka-Seltzer, adhesive bandage, hair cream or Aspirin for 10¢
- Electric shaver for 25¢ ("Burglar alarm will sound if shaver cord is cut")
- 10¢ Mechanical Shoeshiner ("Important: raise legs of trousers first")
- machine on which you can punch out Metal-type Identification Medal (i.e. your name) at 32 letters for 10¢
- a very curious machine which offers Transparent Plastic Protection around photos or licenses in 10 seconds
- a 5¢ Relax-a-lator (foot massage machine)
- 25¢ Take Your Own Photo booth
- a Gripmeter—"Improve Your Grip on Life"
- The Lord's Prayer as a Lucky Charm Medal 10¢
- a Sellomatic machine dispensing Skeleton

68

Fingers, Puzzles, Dolly's Telescope, Plastic
Field-glasses and Shrunken Heads for 25¢
- a Face-Tone Machine—"Look Alive, Feel
  Alive. The 3-minute aid to smart Grooming.
  Equivalent of 2½ hours of sunshine in 3 minutes. Gives you a healthy sun-drenched glow
  for that important appointment ahead of you."
  —25¢

- 30 stalls (nearly always full to overflowing)
- 60 toilets approached through 10¢ turnstile
- 8 h. & c. basins (use of proper towel, 5¢)
- 30 dressing rooms with own toilet at 25¢
- 30 dressing rooms with shower and toilet at
  75¢

Restrictions in here: No Shaving at Basins. No Loitering (Violators Liable to Arrest)— which seems a little bit hard when so many diversions have been laid on that encourage lighthearted loitering.

B. The Lower Level Johns (open 7 a.m. to 11 p.m.)

Women: 15 toilets (13 at 10¢, 2 free), 16 h. & c. basins, outer room and dispensers as upstairs.

Men: 3 shoeshine seats, 14 stalls, 16 toilets at 10¢ and 1 free, 14 h. & c. basins (5¢ for towel and soap), pay phones. And in an adjacent room, 11 25¢ private washrooms with electric shaver outlet over the basins, and soap and towel in plain brown sealed envelope. This is a pretty high-class joint patronized mostly by the Pullman set.

The UN-AMERICAN JOHNS

United Nations (General Assembly) Building, First Ave. at end of 45th St.

Open: 9:00 to 5:45

Technically these johns are not on American soil at all, and punishment for the normal sort of offenses you can commit in American johns—standing on seats, combing your hair over sinks, etc.—would become a complicated matter for the UN to deal with. The johns are downstairs in the main concourse near the UN Coffee Shop. **Women:** 14 free toilets and 11 h. & c. basins. **Men:** 10 stalls, 5 free toilets, 6 h. & c. basins. Both sets fairly clean and unremarkable.

★★The WALDORF-ASTORIA or ONCE GREATEST JOHNS ON EARTH

Waldorf-Astoria Hotel, 301 Park Ave. (between E. 49th and E. 50th Sts.)

Near the main entrance:

Women: An elegant outer room with sofa, chairs, tables and chandelier. Curved staircase leading up from it to a series of 8 little private rooms each containing free toilet, h. & c. basin and mirror. Tip 25¢.

Men: Mock Regency outer room in which no gentleman would feel ashamed to pass his time of day; leading into a room with 4 stalls (always the chance of rubbing shoulders with foreign dignitaries), 3 free toilets, 4 h. & c. basins (attendant fills them for you, hands you your towel). **Free extras:** Alka-Seltzer, Bufferin, hair lotions and tonics, talcs, small electric shoe polisher and soft music. Tip 25¢.

Only grand in an adequate sort of way. We'd expected to be more impressed. These were, after all, once described as The Greatest Johns on Earth.

JOHNS OF THE
WEST FIFTIES

★★★★LOS JOHNDAS DEL SOL

La Fonda del Sol Restaurant, 123 W. 50th St. (between Sixth and Seventh Aves.)

Open: Daily noon to 1 a.m.

Here we have some of the gayest johns in town.

Women: (turn left inside the entrance and up the stairs) Outer room has Bernique Longley's splendid Mexican-style mural in it—known, we understand, in a hurried sort of way, by not a few of the place's male clientele. Inner room has 4 free toilets, 2 h. & c. basins with taps that look like extremely inedible blue and orange mushrooms.

Men: (downstairs inside the entrance) Terrifically elegant room. 4 stalls, 3 free toilets (book matches supplied with the inset ashtrays), 3 h. & c. basins with fun taps, 2 dressing tables like the Women have. **Free extras:** shaver, nail clippers, various colognes and talcs. Restrictions: the Positively No Dancing Allowed on the Tables on Sundays rule also applies to the fittings here.

SAITO'S JAPANESE JOHN

Saito Restaurant, 131 W. 52nd St. (between Sixth and Seventh Aves.)

Open: noon to 3, 5:30 to 11:30, closed Sun.

The **Ladies' Room** on the 2nd floor is the only one we saw in New York outside the door of which were lined up 6 pairs of men's shoes. That was enough for us. **Men's Room** around the corner.

The "21" JOHNS

"21" Club, 21 West 52nd St. (between Fifth and Sixth Aves.)

We were told at the door we couldn't use them unless we had reservations.

The AMERICANA JOHNS

Americana Hotel, 811 Seventh Ave. (between W. 52nd and W. 53rd Sts.)

Always we get the impression in these hotels that can accommodate several thousand persons that we must be missing out on some vast 100- or 500-seater sets of johns where they all go.

Here for instance we found 4 free toilets for women and 4 for men on the first floor, a further 8 for women and 6 for men in the basement. For these to be considered adequate, guests would surely have to visit them in a rota system.

There are some pretty blue mosaic walls in the downstairs **Women's Room,** and an abundance of after-shave lotions and the like above the basins in the **Men's.** Also on a shelf in the first-floor **Men's** is what we believe to be the only bottle of antiseptic mouthwash gargle offered to patrons of any New York john.

The JOHNS OF THE SIXES

Top of the Sixes, 666 Fifth Ave. (between 52nd and 53rd Sts.)

There's absolutely no point in visiting johns on top of a building like this if they don't have a view. These don't.

The MUSEUM OF MODERN JOHNS

Museum of Modern Art, 11 West 53rd St. (between Fifth and Sixth Aves.)

Open: Mon. to Sat. 11 to 6 (Thurs. 11 to 9), Sun. 12 to 6. Admission $1

There are a number of small galleries where permanent exhibitions of contemporary toilets are on view:

A. Through the cafeteria on the main floor, these galleries concentrate on exhibits of a strictly functional nature. We feel they could be exhibited to better advantage in less cramped surroundings.

B. On the main floor by Gallery 3, two small collections of ceramic art which make an exciting use of form and water. (Note: the doors leading into these rooms have no handle, or title. The only indication that they are doors is the grubby hand marks on them. Some people stand in front of them and study their catalogues unsuccessfully for some reference to them; others just stand and stare at them and try to puzzle out their meaning on their own.)

C. On the lower level by the auditorum, the mural in the **Men's** Exhibition Room, making an exciting use of blue tiles, is of particular interest; also the arrangement of the toilets, two of which face each other—the only known example of this unknown American artist's work.

D. On the 2nd floor opposite Gallery 20 a small Exhibition of more interest to **Women,** but to be appreciated properly and as they were intended to be, some of the exhibits should undergo cleaning.

E. On the 3rd floor just before the Sculpture Galleries a daring **Men-Only** Exhibition including a number of stalls on loan from the collection of Mrs. E. G. Pallberger and other surrealist works including the celebrated panel "Closet."

If you are planning on using these johns frequently it is more economical to pay an annual membership fee—$22 a year for residents of New York, $18 for nonresidents —which confers free admission at all times.

The DONNELL JOHNS

Donnell Library, 20 West 53rd St. (between Fifth and Sixth Aves.)

Open: 9–9 Mon. to Fri., 9–6 Sat.

Nothing very exceptional about these but we should point them out as a free alternative to the costly Modern Art johns over the road. Though even here one of the 3 **Men's** toilets costs 5¢. **Women:** 6 free.

The EARLY AMERICAN FOLK JOHNS

Museum of Early American Folk Arts, 49 W. 53rd St. (between Fifth and Sixth Aves.)

Open: daily except Mon. 10:30 to 5:30. Admission 25¢

Doors not marked but they're the ones opposite the ticket and souvenir desk on the 2nd floor. Only opened in 1963, these small johns are still struggling to build up a regular clientele.

The HILTON JOHNS

New York Hilton Hotel, 1335 Sixth Ave. (between 53rd and 54th Sts.)

There's one set of johns at the end of the basement Concourse, another on the first floor along the Rue des Gourmets. They're all exactly what you'd expect.

The PRIMITIVE JOHNS

Museum of Primitive Art, 15 W. 54th St. (between Fifth and Sixth Aves.)

Open: Tues.–Sat. 12 to 5, Sun. 1 to 5. Admission 50¢

Small **Primitive Men's John** and small **Primitive Women's John** through a pale blue curtain on ground floor rear.

The GOTHAM JOHNS

Gotham Hotel, 700 Fifth Ave. (corner of 55th St.)

Women: (turn right inside 55th St. entrance, follow sign pointing to L'Interdit Discothèque. Take the door marked **Powder Room** just before it.) 2 free toilets (mother-of-pearl seats, shaving outlets above each), 1 h. & c. basin.

Men: (continue right and take staircase going down. Door halfway down it bearing silhouette of French gendarme's head.) 2 stalls, 2 free toilets, 2 h. & c. basins, 1 chair, dizzy-making black and white tiles on the floor.

★★HENRI BENDEL'S PRETTY LADIES JOHNS
w

Henri Bendel (Department Store) 10 W. 57th St. (between Fifth and Sixth Aves.)

Small elegant premises (2 free toilets, 1 h. & c. basin) on the 2nd floor back, near the dressing rooms (but door totally unmarked), catering almost exclusively for ladies with lithe, slim figures up to Size 12.

The BERGDORF-GOODMAN JOHNS

Bergdorf-Goodman, Ladies Apparel, 754 Fifth Ave. (corner of W. 58th St.)

Women: There are rooms on the 3rd floor (turn right out of the lift and go to the back), and the 5th floor (by the Ski Shop). But the best one is undoubtedly that on the 4th floor behind the Antiques department. 2 free toilets, 1 h. & c. basin and everything very clean and yellow except the soap bar which is clean and white.

Men: A fairly civilized single-seater job on the 4th floor through Antiques.

HUNTINGTON HARTFORD'S JOHNS

Gallery of Modern Art, 2 Columbus Circle (corner of
W. 59th St. and Central Park West)

Open: Tues.–Sat. 11 to 7, Sun. 12 to 6.

These johns belong to Huntington Hartford who has seen
fit to house them in his art collection here and charge

$1 admission. Going from top to bottom, there's one **Women's Room** approached down some steps from the 5th floor; another by the Dalis on the 2nd floor. A **Men's Room** between the 1st and 2nd floors. And johns for both down off the basement auditorium. None of them reflect anything except a rather dull and hygienic taste in johns from their owner (perfectly clean though).

The PLAZA JOHNS (incorporating the Palm Court Johns, the Persian Johns, the Edwardian Johns, the Oak Johns, Trader Vic's Johns and Julius Monk's Johns)

The Plaza Hotel, Fifth Ave. and W. 59th St. immediately below Central Park

A. The 1st-Floor Johns (serving the Palm Court, Persian Room and Edwardian Room)

Women: (directly to right of Fifth Ave. entrance) Outer room with sofa, chairs, blue carpet and pay phones. Side room with counters, mirrors and stools for makeup (but not well lighted at all). Inner sanctum with 5 free toilets, 5 h. & c. basins (real soap and sponges provided at each, and attendant hovering with linen towels). **Free extras:** Kleenex and perfumes. Tip 25¢.

Men: (to the right inside entrance) Basically it's 3 stalls, 2 free toilets, 3 h. & c. basins. But then there's an attendant who says "Hello! How are you?" as you come in and points to whatever stall or basin may be free, and later hands you a towel and brushes you down. It makes a change from the subway. **Free extras** on the shelf over the basins: Vaseline Hair Tonic, brush and comb, Jeris Talc, Westphal's After-shave Lotion, Lilac Vegetal, Vitalis, Dandruff Remover, pad of paper. Tip 25¢.

B. The Basement Johns (serving the Oak Room, Trader Vic's and Julius Monk's Plaza 9)

Women: (off Trader Vic's lobby) Outer room for makeup and chaise-longueing, inner room with 5 free toilets, 5 h. & c. basins. **Free extras:** hand lotion and Kleenex. Tip 25¢.

Men: (in the passageway) A well-equipped establishment, this. Shoeclean service. 4 free toilets, 5 stalls, 4 h. & c. basins, even a bench you can write at. **Free extras:** clothesbrush, scrubbing brush, Kleenex, Hair Fertilizer, Mennen Shave Talc, Vi-Jon Hair Cream, Stephan Lilac Toilet Water—and above all, Alka-Seltzer, Bromo-Seltzer, Bufferin, Aspirin. Tip 25¢ and tell the man he's doing a good job.

JOHNS OF THE
EAST FIFTIES

The CRANE COMPANY'S NO-JOHN

Crane Company, Park Ave. (between 50th and 51st Sts.)

This is the showroom of the people who appear to make the majority of the toilet fittings described in this book. Despite the impressive display of similar toilets and basins in their windows they have none that may be used either by the public or by their own smiling salesmen, who when in dire need must travel to the 9th floor of an adjacent building. Plumber, plumb thyself etc.

★★★The JOHNS OF THE FOUR SEASONS

The Four Seasons Restaurant, 99 E. 52nd St. (between Park and Lexington Aves.)

Open: noon to 1 a.m., closed Sun.

Naturally they're very grand, with masses of marble and rosewood, everything gleaming, but somehow lacking an air of being *lived in*. The **Women's Room** with a fine array of perfumes and makeup articles free for the using is to the left of the entrance hall. The **Men's Room,** with equal benefits and the smartest attendant in the world to dispense them, to the right. Features of both johns, which we haven't encountered elsewhere, are the push-button flushers set into the floor beside each toilet (surprising results if you don't notice them the first time), and the inset ashtrays and marble reading lamps on the walls to the side of the toilets. A pity they don't go the whole hog and install telephones too.

DAWSON'S JOHNS

Dawson's Restaurant and Bar, 159 East 53rd St. (between Third and Lexington Aves.)

This place sets out to be an imitation of an Old English pub. One thing which lets the Old English image badly down: all the plumbing in the john works.

★ The BOAT HOUSE JOHNS

Boat House Bar, 167 E. 54th St. (off Third Ave.)

It's great to stumble across (if not into) a small place like this which has made some effort to dress its johns up. They're nothing fantastic, the rooms are simply done in the same sort of rough wood as the rest of the premises; but the white porcelain of the toilet fittings looks splendid against such a background. One criticism: the door leading into the **Men's Room** is about the narrowest we've ever stumbled across (if not through). It must certainly limit the shape of clients who can visit the room.

In fact upon reflection it must be the narrowest door we've ever seen. Possibly in the whole of New York.

The ST. REGIS JOHNS

St. Regis Hotel, 2 East 55th St. (just around the corner from Fifth Ave.)

Women: (turn left through a brocade curtain at top of steps by hotel entrance nearest to Madison

Ave.) 2 free toilets each in its own room, 2 h. & c. basins (real soap), old French fashion prints around the walls.

Lord and Lady Saint John

Men: (straight down the stairs opposite this entrance, just past the barbershop) 3 stalls, 2 free toilets 3 h. & c. basins. **Extras:** shaver outlets, shoe-shine chairs (35¢), red carpeting and a lot of marble.

★ **P. J. CLARKE'S JOHNS**

M

P. J. Clarke's Bar at Third Ave. and 55th St.

Open: Until about 4 a.m.

Women: 1) Off the back room, 1 free toilet, 1 h. & c. basin, revolving towel and mirror. Very tiny: if someone else opens the door while you're at the basin there's no way to avoid a doorknob in your back except to be under three feet high. Then, watch your head.

2) Off the front room, toilet and basin in the same brown and mustard colored room and a bolt on the door ensures both an old-fashioned privacy and immunity from knobs.

Men: At the back end of the front room. 1 fairly recent h. & c. basin with two linen roller towels, 2 of the oldest and biggest stalls in New York both lined with great hunks of ice, 2 equally splendid toilets with mahogany partitions and near-Gothic swing doors. (On the wall of one is carved the legend "Ray Milland was here" and underneath that is written "So was Fergie." And on the wall of the other, at the time of our visit, was scrawled, not carved, the familiar slogan "Abramowitz is a Neo-Classicist" underneath which another pen had written "Bullshit. He's a fairy.") With its green glass window, its mahogany, and its rounded stained-glass roof this is a must for every visitor to New York whether he feels in need of it or not. The sign on the wall "Please Open Door Slowly" is to discourage you from knocking over passing waiters on your way out. (But despite this and the knob in the Women's Room it's not really a violent place.)

86

The TIFFANY JOHNS

Tiffany & Co., Jewelers, 727 Fifth Ave. (between 56th and 57th Sts.)

Women: (elevator to mezzanine and turn left) 3 free toilets, 3 h. & c. basins (real soap). Carpeted outer room contains enormous mirror, makeup tables, sofa, chairs, desk with inter-store phone to make ordering diamonds easier, 2 pay phones in wood-paneled booths. Attendant, who is fond of referring to the people who come in here as *her* customers, and who has a happy greeting for all her regulars, keeps the place in a far better state than many first-class hotels. "I have my customers well-trained," she explains.

Men: (elevator to 6th floor, turn left through what seems to be somebody's office) 4 stalls, 4 free toilets, 3 h. & c. basins. Just not on a par with the Women's Room. And also, we strongly suspect we saw a jeweler in it.

The SCHWARZ JOHNS

F. A. Schwarz, Toys, 745 Fifth Ave. (between 58th and 59th Sts.)

Either they've catered for outsize children and toddlers in the johns here, or else not catered for children at all. Not even a potty in sight.

Women (or Outsize Girls): in the Baby Bazaar, 2nd floor.
Men (or Outsize Boys): 2nd floor through Accounting.

BLOOMINGDALE'S BARGAIN JOHNS

Bloomingdale's (Department Store), Lexington Ave. at E. 59th St.

Open: Mon.–Sat. 9:30 to 6 (Mon., Thurs. to 9)

Women: 1) In the Downstairs store by the elevators. 29 free toilets, 14 h. & c. basins. Clean, spacious living.
2) In Subway level by Budget Dresses, 9 toilets (5 free, 4 at 10¢), 7 h. & c. basins.

Men: In the Downstairs store through Ladies Stockings, 6 free toilets (all of them a good four inches lower than any other model we've seen, but doctors will advise you this is a far healthier level to live on), room for 5 standing, and 3 h. & c. basins.

BLOOMINGDALE'S UPSTAIRS JOHNS

Women: 1) By the Beauty Salon on the 4th Floor, 35 toilets (18 free and 17 at 10¢—which you can't charge to your account apparently), 19 h. & c. basins, ample makeup ledges and mirrors. **Extras:** 7 pay phones, 2 coin-changing machines.
2) Near the Snack Shop on the 7th Floor, 10 toilets (5 free and 5 at 10¢), 7 h. & c. basins.

Men: Accommodation for 6 seated (low and free) and 4 standing (we were told that Bloomingdale's gives gold plates to favored customers of long standing) and 3 h. & c. basins.

What we can't make out in many establishments like this is by what rule they decide how many toilets shall be free and how many shall be paying ones. Very rarely is there any difference in the fittings of the two, and yet our experience is that few women will go into a free one if there are other women watching or present; men don't seem to mind so much who knows that they may have been using a free john.

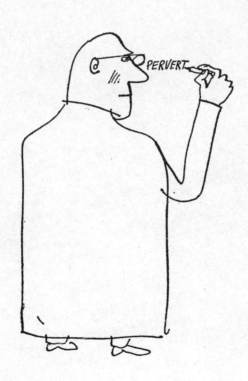

WEST SIDE JOHNS

The UNDERWATER JOHNS

The Circle Line boat that makes the Round Trip of Manhattan, Pier 81 opposite W. 41st St.

If you have a yen, or even a mild hankering, to go to the only john in New York that is below water level, if you're prepared to spend three hours in it (but not any three hours between November 14 and April 3) or if you get your kicks out of being in a john that's traveling at a steady 10 knots an hour, and if you're willing to spend $2.75 for the experience ($1.25 if you're under 12), then these are the johns for you. 3 toilets and 2 cold water basins in the **Women's.** 2 stalls, 2 toilets, and 2 cold water basins in the **Men's.** Very, very clean at the beginning of each trip.

The BUS TERMINAL JOHNS

Port Authority Bus Terminal, between Eighth and Ninth Aves. and 41st and 42nd Sts.

Open: 24 hours

The principal johns here are off the large waiting room on the Main Concourse.

Women: 22 toilets at 10¢, 4 free, 4 dressing rooms (incorporating toilets) at 25¢, 2 shower rooms at 50¢ (soap, towel and bathmat supplied, but best to bring your own mobcap), 20 h. & c. basins. Outer room with makeup area, chairs, tables and Honest Weight machines.

Men: 4 shoeshine chairs at 25¢, 16 stalls, 14 10¢ toilets and 1 free, 11 h. & c. basins (soap dispenser and paper towel free, or soap bar and linen towel 10¢). **Extras:** 5 dressing rooms (incorporating toilets) at 25¢, Shower Room 50¢, Bathroom 50¢. Restrictions: No Loitering. No Shaving Permitted at Wash Basins.

There are also lesser sets of johns on the floor above and the floor below.

The WEST SIDE MUSICAL JOHNS

West Side Air Terminal, corner of Tenth Ave. and 42nd St.

Open: 24 hours

These are as good value as you get in anything at this end of 42nd Street. Both up the stairs off Main Concourse.

Women: Inner room, 9 toilets (1 free, 8 at 10¢), 9 h. & c. basins. **Extras:** Soft music; lipstick dispenser 25¢. Outer room, makeup tables and stools. **Extras:** Baby's Crib; 25¢ dispenser giving choice of Nail Clippers, Aspirin, Handkerchief, Toothbrush, Comb, Perfume.

Men: 7 stalls, 10 toilets (1 free, 9 at 10¢), 7 h. & c. basins (no restrictions on shaving). **Extras:** Soft music; penny scale; 25¢ Automatic Merchant ("Report Malfunction") selling Quality Handkerchief, Shave Cream Cartridge, Vaseline Hair Tonic, Razor, Aspirin, Ball-point Pen, Comb, Nail Clippers, ¼ fl. oz. "Delilah" Perfume. Also shoeshine and parcel room attached. Nine out of ten for cleanliness.

JIM DOWNEY'S JOHNS

Jim Downey's Steak House, 705 Eighth Ave. (between 44th and 45th Sts.)

Open: 11:30 a.m. to 3:00 a.m. daily

The seats in the **Men's** light up.

The YWCA JOHNS

YWCA (West Side Branch) on 51st St. at Eighth Ave.

Open: 24 hours (but No Bums)

Best to ask the doorman how to reach them; somewhere down in the basement.

Young Women: 6 free toilets, 3 h. & c. basins, largish side room with makeup ledges, mirrors and wicker chairs.

Young Men: 4 stalls, 5 free toilets, 2 h. & c. basins. Clean if a bit dilapidated, but as you've got very little right to be here in the first place it's a little ungallant to complain.

The PIER 92 JOHNS

Pier 92 (Cunard Co.), Twelfth Ave. opposite end of 52nd St.)

Open: 9 to 5 a couple of days a week whenever one of the *Queens* or some other Cunarder is in port. See paper for dates.

Women: (to right of north elevator on Boarding Level) 4 free toilets, 3 h. & c. basins, drinking fountain. Outer room with sofa, chairs, table and sewing

93

machine (unless, of course, someone had just left it there that day).

Men: (berthing side of Boarding Level) 4 stalls, 4 free toilets, 3 h. & c. basins. Outer room with 2 sofas, 4 wheelchairs, and a view through the window of the *Queen Mary*'s bows the day we were there.

The other piers belonging to the larger shipping companies have similar facilities. Watch papers for dates of liners docking. And some liners allow you aboard at certain times to use their johns.

THE JOHNS
OF CENTRAL PARK

Wherever you go in the Park you're not far from a john. There are 20 sets altogether, not all of which you might care to be seen in. We recommend the ones below:

A. **The Zoo Loos (or Zoological Johns)** off Fifth Ave. opposite E. 64th St. The **Women's Room** (next to the Grizzly Bear, or *Ursus horribilis,* and for goodness sake don't get the doors mixed up) has 9 free toilets for people and 2 for children, and 7 h. & c. basins (but bring your own soap and towel). The **Men's Room** by the Polar Bear has 13 stalls, 8 free toilets, 7 h. & c. basins. Restrictions: No Bicycle Riding. No Roller Skating. No Dogs. But both are quite clean and well kept.

B. **The Wollman Memorial Johns** on the esplanade over the skating rink. The entrances are marked **Boys** and **Girls** but take no notice. Same restrictions apply as for the Zoo and also No Peddling.

C. More extensive johns actually on rink level but you need to pay 50¢ admission to reach them. They also have dressing rooms (for changing out of your bicycling, roller-skating or peddling costume; for changing into your ice gear).

D. Over on the other side of the Park, not far from the West 67th St. entrance, the **Tavern-on-the-Green Johns** (open noon to 1 a.m. daily). Here are free toilets, and the soap and towels which may have eluded you at other Park establishments.

I could be wrong but I think I've discovered what this was originally intended for.

JOHNS WEST
OF CENTRAL PARK

The HISTORICAL JOHNS

New York Historical Society (Museum) 170 Central
Park West (corner of W. 77th St.)

Open: Tues.–Sun. 1 to 5, Sat. 10 to 5. Free admission.

Turn left inside the entrance, then right along a corridor.
Small adequate johns opposite a print depicting "Con-
flagration of the Steamboat Lexington in Long Island
Sound, Monday eve Jan 13th 1840 by which Melancholy
Occurrence OVER 120 PERSONS PERISHED."

Here if anywhere is surely where a few Early American
and historical johns could have been put on view, if not
actually into use. But there's nothing. Would anyone care
to donate a few prints or plans of early johns to hang on
the empty walls of the johns here as a starter to remedy-
ing this sad state?

The NATURAL HISTORY JOHNS

American Museum of Natural History, Central Park
West (between 77th and 81st Sts.)

Open: Weekdays 10 to 5, Sun. 1 to 5. Admission
free.

Many people are put off visiting the johns here because they find them so difficult to locate. On your own they certainly are and you would be mad to try to get through all of them inside of one day. We submit that the easiest way to become familiar with them is to make up a party and reserve a guide to show you around them. But failing that, try and memorize these details:

A. **The 2nd-Floor Johns.** If you enter the Museum from Central Park West (which will put you on the 2nd floor, remember; not the 1st) turn left and walk a mile or so through South Asiatic Mammals. When you hear strange jungle noises and parrots screeching you will know you are getting warm. These noises come from the Men of the Montana Gallery just before which, opposite the case containing the Saiga Antelope, are the johns. Free and very clean, this set. (In fact they're all free here.)

B. **The 1st-Floor Johns.** These are just off the 77th St. foyer, though there is little hope of finding them if you are already inside the building. There are totem poles immediately outside the **Ladies,** and the Museum Shop by the **Men's.** There are 16 free toilets in the **Women's Room** and a penny scale which confides "Weigh in privacy—no one can see your weight but yourself." People come from the farthest ends of the five boroughs to use it. The **Men's Room** is a very spacious one and one might inquire whether it can be hired for holding a dance in.

C. **The Subway-Level Johns,** on the floor below the 1st floor. All we can say is that these definitely do exist, just off a very large waiting room.

D. **The 3rd-Floor Johns.** We deny that there are any.

E. **The 4th-Floor or Prehistoric Johns.** Approaching this floor by the stairway turn right by Juvenile Mastodontines and they're opposite the skeleton of the Long-Jawed Megabelodon. Approaching from any other way, give up; leave the Museum if you can even find an Exit and go to the Historical Museum next door.

The HEAVENLY JOHNS

Hayden Planetarium, Central Park West on 81st St. (around the corner from the Natural History Museum)

This is a costly business. $1 during the day, $1.25 in the evenings. And for that our female department got about the dirtiest, messiest, ugliest john she'd visited in a public building. The **Men's Room** wasn't so bad. (Someone, or possibly himself, had scrawled "Fidel Castro was here" in our toilet.) To find them (if you have to): turn right inside the 81st St. entrance and go downstairs. Or if you enter from the Natural History Museum the Viking Rocket exhibit is pointing in the right direction. And neither room has any view, let alone of the night sky. We would recommend, if this is your interest, biding your time and finding a quiet place outside where only the stars need be witness to your needs.

The PEEPING JOHNS

Broadway and 96th St., on an island in the middle of the road

Open: *Very*. Indeed some people seem to spend their day just crossing backward and forward over the road for peeping's sake. Go there yourself between 8 A.M. and 7 P.M. (or 9 A.M. and 6 P.M. weekends) and maybe you'll see the attraction.

Women: 5 free toilets (bring your own seat though), 1 h. & c. basin but the h. doesn't work and there's no soap or towel. Despite these setbacks the attendant makes a laudable effort to keep the place clean.

Men: 9 stalls, 6 free toilets, 1 cold-water basin.

JOHNS EAST
OF CENTRAL PARK

The SERENDIPITY JOHNS

Serendipity 3, 225 E. 60th (between Second and Third Aves.)

Open: 11 a.m. to 1 a.m. Mon.–Sat.

Women: (stained-glass door on the left halfway down the shop with an "L" on it) 1 free toilet (pull-chain flush), 1 tiny basin, old prints on the wall.

Men: (similar door marked "G") 1 free toilet (overhead cistern and gold chain), 1 tiny corner basin, old, old mirror.

All these fittings, including the doors, are for sale. (They also sell in the shop perforated toilet tissue printed like bank notes, and The Washroom Wise-Saying Kit—"handsome collection of assorted stickers designed to satisfy the gentleman's need for creative self-expression when visiting a public john, a genteel gift for the busy man who hasn't got time to scribble something on the washroom wall."—"Abramowitz is a Neo-Classicist" turns up on it, too. It may, of course, all be a sinister government plot to control the quality and content of graffiti.)

101

★★★★HENRY C. FRICK'S JOHNS

The Frick Museum, Fifth Ave. and E. 70th St.

Open: Tues.–Sat. 10 to 6, Sun. 1 to 6, closed Mon. Admission free.

These johns, sharing a joint entrance in the front hall, must be ranked among the most elegant in New York; and in their own field their fittings are the equal of any of the other splendid treasures collected by Frick and on show elsewhere in the building.

Women: 3 free toilets, 3 h. & c. basins, outer room for dressing tables that has close carpeting, mirrored walls, chandeliers and an exquisitely executed "No Smoking" sign. There couldn't be a nicer room to change in before a Ball, or even to have as one's address for the Season.

Men: 3 stalls and 3 free toilets in one room (pull-down seat lids that automatically flush the bowl), 3 h. & c. basins in an outer room that seems more suitable for entertaining. And absolutely spotless.

Any visitor to the johns of New York should place the Frick johns right near the top of his list. It may of course be the effect of the fountains in the main hallway but most visitors to the Museum proper do inquire after them anyway.

The PARKE-BERNET JOHNS

Parke-Bernet Galleries, 980 Madison Ave., between 77th and 78th Sts.

Open: Wed.–Sat. 10 to 5, Tues. 10 to 7, closed Sun. and Mon.

Women: Elevator to the 3rd floor and turn left, 2 free

toilets, 2 h. & c. basins with ledge and mirror over. Clean and very dull.

Men: Turn right out of elevator on 3rd floor. 2 stalls, 1 free toilet, 2 h. & c. basins. Clean, but nothing you'd really want to bid for.

The METROPOLITAN MUSEUM JOHNS

Fifth Ave. and 82nd St. on the Park.

Open: Mon.–Sat. 10 to 5, Sun. and holidays 1 to 5. Admission free.

A. Main Floor. The **Greek-Roman Johns.** Turn left through the Main Entrance (5th Ave. and 82nd St.) and make for the Restaurant, and left again when you come up against the base of some vast column. You should now pass, on the wall, an exhibit entitled "Colossal Limestone head of a Warrior, 600 B.C." and also a notice just before you reach the johns saying "Occupancy by more than 444 persons is dangerous and unlawful." (Though this may not refer to the johns. Just to be on the safe side, if there are that many of you, split up and let some of the party visit the other johns.)

Women: 4 free toilets, 5 h. & c. basins with makeup ledge and mirrors.
Men: 2 stalls, 2 free toilets, 2 h. & c. basins.

B. Main Floor. The **French 18th-Century Johns.** Quite difficult to find. At the back of the building from the main entrance, not far from the Louis XVI Room. Nearest noticeable exhibit: the not inappropriately placed Great Malachite Pot of the Demidoffs.

Women: 5 free toilets, 3 h. & c. basins, ledges and mirrors, 1 drinking fountain.
Men: 6 stalls, 3 h. & c. basins, 5 free toilets. Clean and very un-French.

C. Second Floor. The **Special Exhibition Johns.** Through Greek and Etruscan Vases if you're approaching from this floor; or, at the head of the stairs leading from the Greek-Roman Johns below.

Women: 4 free toilets, 2 h. & c. basins, ledges and mirrors.
Men: 4 stalls, 2 free toilets, 2 h. & c. basins.

D. Ground Floor. The **Costume Institute Johns.** These are directly opposite the entrance on 83rd St.

Women: Outer room with drinking fountain and makeup counter and mirror. Inner room, 3 free toilets, 2 h. & c. basins.

Men: Outer room of singular gloom and bleakness, containing one very wide bench eminently suited for resting a coffin on and having people file past. Inner room, by comparison madly gay, with 3 free toilets, 2 stalls, 2 h. & c. basins.

E. Ground Floor. The **Junior Johns.** Not far from the 81st St. entrance in the Junior Museum. Marked **Boys** and **Girls** but no special tiny fittings.

All the johns in this museum are reasonably clean, and yet completely characterless. Of no interest to collectors.

FRANK LLOYD WRIGHT'S SEMICIRCULAR AND CURIOUSLY CURVED JOHNS

The Solomon R. Guggenheim Museum, 1071 Fifth Ave. (between 88th and 89th Sts.)

Open: Tues.–Sat. 10 to 6 (to 9 Thurs.), Sun. noon to 6. Admission 50¢

Frank Lloyd Wright always designed controversial johns, and these, which are not the least among the exhibits on display here, are no exception. Built one on top of the other, on each floor of the curving ramp inside the building, each contains similar fittings—one basin, one toilet. The **Women's** are semicircular, the **Men's** defy all simple explanation so far as their shapes go—note, too, the cunning differences between the one on the ground floor and those above. 50¢ may seem an exorbitant admission fee but if you spread your visits out among the 5 johns available to each sex, it works out at the standard 10¢ each. One complaint: no reproductions of these johns are on sale at the desk in the entrance lobby.

The JEWISH JOHNS

The Jewish Museum, 1109 Fifth Ave. (corner of 92nd St.)

Open: Mon.–Thurs., noon to 5, Fri. 11 to 3, Sun. 11 to 6

These johns are run by the Jewish Theological Seminary of America. There is a **Women's Room** on the 2nd floor near the elevators and a **Men's Room** on the stairs between 1st and 2nd floors, both of which contain a number of ritual vessels more chaste than ornate; and a complete set of johns in the basement outside the door of which is a Mystical 10¢ Pretzel Stix Machine. Use them on Monday when admission is free (other days one has to pay 50¢ to enter the building).

The EXTRAORDINARY MEN and WOMEN'S BASEMENT JOHNS

Museum of the City of New York, Fifth Ave. at 103rd St.

Open: Tues.–Sat. 10 to 5, Sun. 1–5; closed Mon. Free admission

Women: Down by elevator to the basement and through what they call the Hose Carriage Room. This is the only Women's Room in the world equipped with a fire engine, as opposed to a mere fire extinguisher. So if you're prone to setting yourself alight make use of the place with confidence. 4 free toilets, 2 h. & c. basins, no mirror but very clean.

Men: By elevator to the basement also and turn through a door beside a picture of "The Burning of the Tombs Cupola by an Angry Mob, 1842." 4 stalls, 3 basins (sometimes h. & c., but sometimes just c.), 4 no-door toilets. Sometimes standing outside this room you get the impression that there's someone inside it playing a piano. They're always gone by the time you get in, though.

The GRACIE MANSION OUTSIDE JOHNS

Small stone outhouse set not far from the Mansion in Carl Schurz Park opposite the end of 87th St.

Open: approx. 8 a.m. to 5 p.m.

Women: 2 free toilets, 1 cold-water sink, no soap or towels.

Men: 2 stalls, 1 free toilet, 1 cold-water basin.

Better luck to the Mayor's guests inside the Mansion. But nice surroundings.

THE JOHNS OF
UPPER MANHATTAN

The ULYSSES S. GRANT JOHNS

Riverside Park, the other side of Riverside Drive to Grant's Tomb (approx. 123rd St.)

Open: Approx. 7:30 to 4:30 daily

Though not host, or an object of pilgrimage, to so many visitors each year this building is, at least externally, the architectural superior to the Tomb across the road, and must rank as one of the most perfect examples of classical john construction in America. Its site too can hardly be bettered. Which all makes a sad lead-up to the state of its interior:

Women: 10 free toilets (no seats and only waist-high doors), 2 cold-water basins (no mirrors, no soap, no towel). Restrictions: No Smoking, Loitering, Dogs or Spitting.

Men: 6 stalls, 10 free toilets (no doors), 1 cold-water basin. Restrictions: No Smoking or Loitering. Beware of Pickpockets. Do not Spit on the Floor. No Dogs Allowed.—Which is about the most Don'ts that have appeared on one tablet since the days of the Ten Commandments.

109

The INADEQUATE INDIAN JOHNS

Museum of the American Indian, off Broadway between 155th and 156th Sts. (first building on the left in the courtyard)

Open: Tues.–Sun. 1 to 5. Admission free

Women: (3rd floor opposite head of stairway, exhibits of the Ceramic Art of Panama outside) More recent examples of the Ceramic Art of the U. S. inside include 3 free toilets and 2 h. & c. basins. Smells very musky.

Men: (through the door marked **Offices** by stairway on 1st floor, near exhibits outside labeled "Apache native fiddle made from yucca stalk" and "Apache Medicine Pouch") 1 free toilet, 1 h. & c. basin.

The johns in this building are about the only things not made by Indians. Unless we overlooked some other rooms they seem totally inadequate to deal with the demands of the 264,375 schoolchildren who entered the building alongside us.

★★★The HISPANIC JOHNS
M

Museum of the Hispanic Society of America, off Broadway between 155th and 156th Sts.)

Open: Tues.–Sat. 10 to 4:30, Sun. 2 to 5. Admission free.

Women: (to right of entrance hall and downstairs) 1 free toilet, 2 h. & c. basins, chaise-longue, very spacious.

Men: (also down the stairs) 2 great stalls, 2 free toilets with Empire-style swing doors in gold and brown against white marble, 1 very fine,

110

very rare double basin. One of the most purely elegant johns in all New York, which makes it all the sadder that we were about the tenth pair of visitors it had received all year.

Do you think I might wash my hands?

Not in MY Lavatory

ST. JOHN'S JOHNS

Cathedral Church of St. John the Divine, Amsterdam Ave. at 112th St.

Open: 7 to 6 daily

Women: (to the left just before hall leading to Exhibit Hall, alternatively to the right just after leaving

111

Exhibit Hall) 3 free toilets, 2 h. & c. fonts. Quite plain, clean and painted baby blue.

Men: (turn left after entering Exhibit Hall from outside; or turn right after entering Exhibit Hall from nave) 3 stalls, 2 free toilets, 2 h. & c. fonts, 1 foot font.

These are the Mother Johns of the Episcopal Church's Diocese of New York and also the only johns in any Cathedral in New York.

★ The JUMEL JOHNS

Jumel Mansion in Roger Morris Park between 160th and 162nd Sts. and Edgcombe Ave.

Open: 11 to 5 daily except Sun., admission free

Different covens of the Daughters of the American Revolution are responsible for the furnishings and upkeep of each room in this splendid colonial mansion, perhaps the most beautiful though least known of all New York's museums. The lot who have custody of the johns don't name themselves, however. Visiting the johns, which are literally soaked in American history, can be quite an adventure on account you're not free to roam around the mansion at will; the curator has to supervise your whereabouts. And thus if the curator is showing a party around the second floor of the house and one member suddenly wants to visit the john, which is downstairs, the curator and all the rest of the party have to come along too. The curator unlocks the door, you go in and transact your business, then come out, rejoin the party and move off again. At any rate such was our experience. But anything that happens to you in these surroundings is pure pleasure. The **Women's Room** is to the right of the entrance by the stairs and contains 1 free toilet, 1 basin. The **Men's Room** is down in the basement by the original kitchen of the mansion, is stone-flagged and has 2 stalls, 1 free toilet, 1 h. & c. basin and 1 h. & c. footbath. There is also a basin and jug in Mary Bowen's Bedroom on the 2nd floor, and a mirror which used to belong to Mme. Jumel in Aaron Burr's room. No toilet fitting of George Washington's stay here remains. The Women's Room was most likely installed by Seth Middleton in 1887 and the Men's Room by General Earle in 1894.

★ The DYCKMAN JOHNS and the DYCKMAN COMMODE

Dyckman House Park and Museum, 4881 Broadway (at 204th St.)

Open each day except Mon. 11 to 5. Admission free.

Women: Ground level beneath the balcony at front of the house. Tiny room (women over 5 ft. 6 in. can't be accommodated with any degree of comfort) with stone walls, stone floor, 1 cold-water sink (no mirror), and 1 free toilet with an ominous little padlocked door right behind it which could be an emergency entranceway for dwarf plumbers, or something far more sinister.

Men: Ground level back of the house, stone floors and walls, beamed ceiling, 1 stall, 1 free toilet, 1 cold-water sink, all cleverly arranged in an area 4 ft. by 4 ft. With its pretty garden outside, the scent of flowers and the song of the birds, this makes an ideal away-from-it-all weekend john.

The toilets and sinks are about the only fittings in this exquisite Dutch farmhouse not dating from 1783 or earlier. Upstairs, however, in the North Bedroom on the

2nd floor, you will observe a small square three-drawer mahogany chest of drawers. But unlike most similar pieces of furniture, the top of this one lifts up, the side comes down, and the interior is revealed as the ingenious hiding place for a chamber pot. And this Dyckman heirloom, dating from about 1780, and given to the City of New York in 1915 by Mrs. Bashford Dean and Mrs. Alexander McMillan Welch in memory of their father, Isaac Michael Dyckman, is the original toilet fitting of the place. Not available for use by the public, though.

The MONASTIC JOHNS

The Cloisters, Fort Tryon Park

Open: Tues.–Sat. 10 to 5, Sun. and Hols. 1 to 5, closed Mon. Admission free.

These johns, which are a branch of the johns in the Metropolitan Museum, were built and presented to the city by John D. Rockefeller, Jr., in 1938. Though set in what appears to be a series of 13th-century monasteries, the only really medieval feature of the johns is the actual approach to them—along ramparts, through meandering stone colonnades, in and out of little chapels, and down the sort of steps that normally lead to dungeons. They're not clearly marked and it may be best to seek the advice of a guide in locating them. And don't panic if you can't find your way out of them because, despite the thought that may occur to you, you're not part of any plot to keep you there against your will, or even to induct you into the church; it's just the way the building's built.

Women: (and if we had a special sign which signified "Subject to Occasional Flooding" we'd use it here) 5 free toilets, 4 h. & c. basins. Restrictions: No Smoking. No Loitering. No Hair Combing.—Presumably this last being in deference to the medieval nuns who certainly never knew premises like this but who were meant to eschew all vanity and pleasures of the flesh and scalp.

Men: 4 stalls, 3 free toilets, 4 h. & c. basins. And if one ignores the temptations of the hot-water tap this can be a monastically clean and simple experience. **Extra:** the strains of recorded medieval music each Tuesday and Sunday afternoon.

JOHNS OF THE BRONX

EDGAR ALLAN POE'S JOHN

Poe Cottage, Grand Concourse and Kingsbridge Road

Open: daily except Mon. 10 to 1 and 2 to 5 (2 to 4 Nov. to April), Sun. 1 to 5. Admission free.

Our initial impression after a brief look inside this small wooden cottage is that Poe could never have had a bath during his years in New York. But the Curator told us there used to be an outhouse over a hole in the ground, and backing up his story one notices there are indeed 2 large holes in the ground just near the cottage. Steps lead down them and one is marked **Men,** the other **Women.**

In the Women: 5 free toilets, 3 cold-water sinks without soap or towels, 2 other rooms each containing similar fittings: 1 basin and 2 toilets, one of which is half the size of the other and without a seat. One can spend a lot of time conjecturing over these.

In the Men: 5 stalls, 4 free toilets without doors, 2 ancient cold-water basins, and 1 footbath in the wall behind which—we would like to think—is immured some 19th-century plumber who Poe discovered making advances to Annabel Lee.

The ZOOLOGICAL COMFORT STATIONS

Bronx Zoo, 185th St. and Southern Blvd., Bronx

Open: 10 to 5 daily. Fri.–Mon. free admission,
Tues.–Thurs. 25¢

**A. The johns *under* the Lion House (entrance down
steps protected by wire netting and bars behind
the Lion House)**

Women: 6 free toilets, 7 h. & c. basins (1 missing Oct.
'65), and printed instructions how to use
penny-operated linen towel cabinet. (Also missing Oct. '65. We must do something about this
pilfering, Miss Hargreaves.) **Extra:** enormous
penny scale (at any rate, still there Oct. '65).
Also side room or annex with 9 further free
toilets, rather smelly but not in a people sort
of way.

Men: 9 stalls, 5 free toilets, 2 h. & c. basins, penny
scale, roped-off annex with 9 more pink-doored
toilets and 2 basins. One of the warmest rooms
in the whole of New York.

**B. The johns off the pathway between Elephants
and Small Mammals**

Women: 18 free toilets (apricot-colored doors and pale
blue partitions), 3 h. & c. basins, penny scale.

Men: 7 free toilets, 3 h. & c. basins, 7 stalls (and a
further 19 sometimes roped off). The attendants on view at these johns are of an especially
good-natured variety which you may touch, pet
or fondle, but not ride. They have three feeding times each day in private, and you may also
buy small packets of stuffs to feed them yourself from kiosks in the Zoo grounds. Although
none have actually been born in the Zoo some

have been here for 20 or 30 years, and when
fully grown may attain a weight of 170 lbs.

C. There are also johns (like the others marked
Comfort Stations) by the Bronxdale and by the
Boston Road entrances to the Zoo.

The VAN CORTLANDT JOHNS

We visited the Van Cortlandt Mansion in Van Cortlandt
Park as, hearing it was run by the Colonial Dames, we
had visions of Rest Rooms marked "Gents and Dames."
But we were told by the caretaker there were no Rest
Rooms at all and directed to a mean building in the park

nearby which turned out to be a Public John with a **Women's Room** padlocked and a **Men's Room** bearing the legend "No Changing of Clothes Allowed." Had we persisted at that point we now gather we could have found unpadlocked premises in which we could have changed any number of clothes down at the Clubhouse of the Van Cortlandt Park Municipal Golf Course.

FALIK
SYMBOL
FUNTAP
that's me

JOHNS JUST OUT
OF TOWN

The CONEY ISLAND or "FUN" JOHNS

Architecturally about the most pleasing building along the whole shore is the one housing the Free Johns, under the Boardwalk at the shore end of W. 15th St. off Surf Avenue. You can also make quite an entrance into them down the curving stone from the Boardwalk. Alternatively, if you're planning an invasion of the coast from seaward, head toward the Roller Coaster, and the Free Johns building is the one sited between signs proclaiming "The Bushman Baths" and "Steve's Famous Clam Bar." Very large inside: **Men** 24 stalls and 20 free toilets. **Women** almost impossible to count. Nice easygoing atmosphere in both though certain sensible printed limitations on your total abandonment. No Dressing or Undressing. No Combing Hair over Sinks. No Loitering. No Bottles.—Bicycling is not exactly encouraged either. Each year these johns are flushed over 26,350,000 times.

If you prefer a more intimate atmosphere and you've got money to spend or a desperate urge to comb your hair over a sink, there's also **Nathan's 5-Cent Johns**—two little rooms situated behind Nathan's Delicatessen on Surf Ave. under a sign saying "Dining Room—Waiter Service." These are open 24 hours in the summer, but seem to close down about 4 P.M. other times.

And again, if you're someone who doesn't count the cost at all, a really big spender, or maybe just want to impress the company you're keeping, why not take her to the **Aquarium Johns?** (Open, usual aquarium times) Pay your 90¢ at the turnstiles, make past the Beluga Whales and Electric Eel, turn right down the stairway opposite tank containing the Atlantic Croaker, French Grunt and Loggerhead. (You'll soon get to recognize these after your first few visits; and who knows, even learn to love them.) Women have 5 free toilets and 3 h. & c. basins. Men, 6 stalls, 3 free toilets, 3 h. & c. basins.

(And just on the subject of fish, there's one public john in London, England, which has a glass cistern over the toilet with goldfish swimming in it. Thinking along similar lines it would take, of course, a very mighty flush indeed to empty the tank containing the Beluga Whales here—but what a spectacle. You could charge $10 to enter a john with that.)

★★★The IDLEWILD or JOHN F. KENNEDY
w **INTERNATIONAL AIRPORT JOHNS**

The johns most in demand and use here are those at the International Arrival Building. For the main ones, take escalator to the 2nd floor and turn left.

Women: (Room 2115, marked **Ladies, Mesdames, Señoras**) Spacious outer room with plenty of tables, chairs, chaise-longues (or possibly chaises-longue, or even couches) has a smart Women's Club atmosphere about it (No gentlemen callers, no entertaining after 10 P.M.). Inner room, 8 toilets (1 free and 7 at 10¢), and 9 h. & c. basins (8 for people, 1 for dwarfs and unfortunates). Adjoining is a nursery for feeding, canning and changing small persons. Open 24 hours, and all terribly clean and spotless.

Men: (Room 2109, marked **Men, Messieurs, Caballeros**) A very jet-age place. 8 stalls including 1 for dwarfs, 6 toilets (1 free and 5 at 10¢), 9 h. & c. basins also including one for dwarfs. It's a spotless place, this, with a pleasant international atmosphere. After using it, alongside all those Messieurs and Caballeros you'll never be really content in using a mere Men's Room anywhere else.

There are also other lesser johns in this building:

A. On the 2nd floor, outside the Golden Door Restaurant to the right of the escalators. All the toilets here are free and sometimes the **Women's Room** is decorated with a real red rose. The **Men's** toilets are fitted with a curious light device over the seats called Hygeaire which "kills airborne bacteria."

B. On the Observation Deck, little johns, but you have to pay 10¢ to get on to the Observation Deck. Music (and dancing for all we know on some nights) in the **Women's Room,** a footbath in the **Men's.**

C. Downstairs again on the first floor, on the far left. Toilets are free. In the **Women's** outer room a chaise-longue and chair set out as though awaiting the arrival of some visiting psychiatrist and patient. And outside the **Men's Room** are stacks and stacks of the telephone directories of all the world. But you can't take one in with you.

All the other terminal buildings at the airport have their johns, and it will probably take you a good half day to work through them all. The main ones at the TWA Building are up the main stairs and turn left. **Women** have 12 toilets (6 free, 6 at 10¢) and 12 h. & c. basins, and a side room nursery. The **Men's Room** has accommodation for 12 standing, 10 seated (5 free and 5 at 10¢), 12 h. & c.

basins (free lotions and use of razor and nail clippers), and shoeshine.

At the Pan-Am Building the **Women's Room** (by Gate 8) has 8 toilets (4 free, 4 at 10¢), 6 h. & c. basins and a 25¢ Vending Machine should you find you need a comb, aspirin, a pen, perfume, hand lotion, toothbrush, toothpaste, or luggage tag. The **Men's Room** (by Gate 7) is of a more intimate size with just 3 stalls, 5 toilets (1 free and 4 at 10¢), 5 h. & c. basins and a similar 25¢ vending machine offering choice of nail clippers, comb, handkerchief, quality toothbrush, pen, aspirin, hair tonic, luggage tag, Emergency Razor and Perfume "For Your Lady."

Splendid though many of the johns are at this airport, and equally useful many of their features, the one which sticks most in our memory is the miniature Japanese garden which has been grown to conceal the entrances to the tiny johns at the Gulf Gasoline Station in the grounds. You'd have to fly a long, long way to find any other John with an immediate exterior of such charming origami, or originality as they say in this country.

INDEX OF SOME RECOMMENDED
FACILITIES

RECOMMENDATION

Please tear out and post to:
The Better John Guide,
200 Madison Ave., N.Y. 16.

I suggest for inclusion in subsequent issues of *The Better John Guide* the following john(s) in New York:

Name ....

Location ....

Description of facilities and times of opening (Please state whether Men's or Women's Room)

General Remarks

Suggestion submitted by ....

Address:

I do/do not wish to have my name printed as recommending this john.